Parliament, party and politics in Victorian Britain

How did parliament operate in the Victorian period? Was it, as is often assumed, a straight precursor of the current two-party model? In this concise and readable new study, T. A. Jenkins explains in full how political parties operated within the Victorian political arena and how this gradually changed in response to the enormous demands being made upon parliament by a rapidly changing society and an expanding electorate.

Contrary to what is normally assumed, he concludes that parliamentary politics did not resolve itself simply into a two-party system of conflict but worked along more complex divisions and alliances. The book also examines in detail the work of the party whips, the world of the ordinary back-bench M.P., and the process by which parliamentary reform occurred.

NEW FRONTIERS IN HISTORY

series editors
Mark Greengrass
Department of History, Sheffield University
John Stevenson
Worcester College, Oxford

This important series reflects the substantial expansion that has occurred in the scope of history syllabuses. As new subject areas have emerged and syllabuses have come to focus more upon methods of historical enquiry and knowledge of source materials, a growing need has arisen for correspondingly broad-ranging textbooks.

New Frontiers in History provides up-to-date overviews of key topics in British, European and world history, together with accompanying source material and appendices. Authors focus upon subjects where revisionist work is being undertaken, providing a fresh viewpoint welcomed by students and sixth-formers. The series also explores established topics which have attracted much conflicting analysis and require a synthesis of the state of the debate.

Published titles

C. J. Bartlett   Defence and diplomacy: Britain and the Great Powers, 1815–1914

Jeremy Black   The politics of Britain, 1688–1800

Michael Braddick   The nerves of state: taxation and the financing of the English state, 1558–1714

David Brooks   The age of upheaval: Edwardian politics, 1899–1914

Carl Chinn   Poverty amidst prosperity: the urban poor in England, 1834–1914

Conan Fischer   The rise of the Nazis

T. A. Jenkins   Parliament, party and politics in Victorian Britain

Keith Laybourn   The General Strike of 1926

Panikos Panayi   Immigration, ethnicity and racism in Britain, 1815–1945

Daniel Szechi   The Jacobites: Britain and Europe, 1688–1788

John Whittam   Fascist Italy

Parliament, party and politics in Victorian Britain

T. A. Jenkins

Manchester University Press

Manchester and New York

distributed exclusively in the USA and Canada by St Martin's Press

Copyright © T. A. Jenkins 1996

Published by Manchester University Press
Oxford Road, Manchester M13 9NR, UK
and Room 400, 175 Fifth Avenue, New York, NY 10010, USA

Distributed exclusively in the USA and Canada
by St Martin's Press, Inc., 175 Fifth Avenue, New York,
NY 10010, USA

British Library Cataloguing-in-Publication Data
A catalogue record for this book is available from the British Library

Library of Congress Cataloging-in-Publication Data
Jenkins, T. A. (Terence Andrew), 1958–
    Parliament, party and politics in Victorian Britain / T. A.
Jenkins.
        p.   cm. — (New frontiers in history)
    Includes bibliographical references (p.   ).
    ISBN 0–7190–4746–3 (alk. paper). — ISBN 0–7190–4747–1 (pbk. :
alk. paper)
    1. Great Britain. Parliament—History—19th century.
2. Political parties—Great Britain—History—19th century.
3. Great Britain—Politics and government—19th century.   I. Title.
II. Series.
JN543.J45   1996
328.41'09'034—dc20   95–30845
                                                                      CIP

ISBN 0 7190 4746 3 *hardback*
      0 7190 4747 1 *paperback*

First published 1996

99 98 97 96 95   10 9 8 7 6 5 4 3 2 1

Printed in Great Britain
by Bell & Bain Ltd, Glasgow

Contents

Acknowledgements

I would like to express my thanks to the archivists at the numerous national and local record offices where I have been allowed to consult manuscript materials. For permission to quote from original documents, I am grateful to the Trustees of the Chatsworth Settlement, the Earl of Derby, the Marquis of Salisbury, the British Library of Political and Economic Science, and the Buckinghamshire Record Office. Professor Hugh Berrington kindly clarified for me a point in his important article in *Parliamentary Affairs*, and Dr Paul Gurowich generously agreed to my drawing information from his unpublished dissertation. The Twenty-Seven Foundation awarded me a research grant, which I am very pleased to acknowledge.

Abbreviations

BL Add MSS	British Library, Additional Manuscripts series
BLPES	British Library of Political and Economic Science, London
HLRO	House of Lords Record Office
NLS	National Library of Scotland, Edinburgh
PRO	Public Record Office, Kew
RO	Record Office

Introduction

The object of this book is to make the case for a rather different approach to the study of British political history, during the Victorian period, from that with which students will probably be familiar. Its focus is primarily on Parliament itself, which, surprising as it may seem, has received comparatively little attention even in textbooks written by specialist political historians. No doubt this can be explained by reference to the prevailing historiographical trends. Many monographs have been produced dealing with what is termed 'high politics', but these tend to concentrate on a much more elevated sphere of activity than Parliament, being interested more in what went on in Cabinet, and in the rivalries and manoeuvrings of an elite group of politicians.[1] A great deal of work has been done, meantime, in the alternative area of 'low politics', where historians have studied popular protest movements, pressure group campaigns, and the details of local politics and electioneering.[2] Both of these approaches have yielded valuable results, but it is argued here that a third dimension to the political process is being left out, which needs to be integrated into future general accounts of Victorian politics.

Parliament was an institution of medieval origin, which had gradually evolved until it became established as a central part of the system of government. In the process, it built up traditions, and developed a distinct character of its own, and even in the nineteenth century this meant that it operated in a way that was at least partially autonomous from the pressures imposed on it from above and below. It is true, for example, that Parliament was becoming increasingly accountable to a wider electorate during our period, but, as we shall see in chapter 4, it had an important part to play in shaping that electorate through the Reform Acts. The point is that Parliament had its own way of doing things, and this book is particularly concerned with the question of how political parties operated within the parliamentary arena, and how this changed in response to the demands being made upon Parliament by a rapidly changing society and an expanding electorate. Chapters 2 and 5 can be read as a connected pair in this respect. Since they do not provide a straightforward narrative account, a chronological summary has been appended for reference purposes. A brief description of Parliament and its procedures has also been provided in the hope that this will assist students when reading about the working of the Constitution in chapter 1, as this is an essential preliminary to what follows.

Political history has not merely survived as a central part of the academic curriculum, but it continues to prove a fertile source of new ideas and perspectives. Indeed, this book is indebted to the substantial body of specialised research which has accumulated over recent years, much of it only accessible in article form, and some of it rather technical in content. The advent of the journal *Parliamentary History*, in 1982, has been a particularly welcome development. Hopefully, it will be possible to prompt students to ask some new questions about a subject that might otherwise seem to be well-trodden ground. Those whose interests chiefly lie in the field of social and cultural history may also find that the study of parliamentary institutions is not entirely irrelevant to them. Chapter 3, for instance, deals with the world of the party whips and the ordinary back-bench Members of Parliament, while one of the subjects in chapter 1 is the way in which a popular image of the Westminster Parliament served as an expression of Britain's self-identity. At a time when the reputation of the British Parliament has reached a low point, with its authority being challenged by the rise of nationalist movements in Scotland and Wales, on the one hand, and by the institutions of the European Union, on the other, an effort of historical imagination is required in order to appreciate that for much of the nineteenth century, and for many years beyond, Parliament enjoyed considerable prestige and was seen as a model which other countries would do well to copy.

Note on party terminology During the 1830s and 1840s the labels 'Liberal' and 'Conservative' gradually came into use in place of the older labels of 'Whig' and 'Tory.' In order to avoid confusion, I have tried to use the newer party names, except when referring to the early 1830s. It should be noted that the terms Whig and Tory never disappeared, and the former term was still commonly used to describe aristocratic Liberals, and sometimes also as a general label for all moderate Liberals.

Notes

1 Examples of this genre of writing include Maurice Cowling, *1867: Disraeli, Gladstone and Revolution* (Cambridge, 1967), Andrew Jones, *The Politics of Reform 1884* (Cambridge, 1972), and A. B. Cooke and John Vincent, *The Governing Passion: Cabinet Government and Party Politics in Britain, 1885–86* (Brighton, 1974). I happily plead guilty to adopting a similar approach in parts of my *Gladstone, Whiggery and the Liberal Party, 1874–1886* (Oxford, 1988).

2 For instance, Asa Briggs (ed.), *Chartist Studies* (London, 1959); Norman McCord, *The Anti-Corn Law League* (London, 1958); Patricia Hollis (ed.), *Pressure from Without in Early-Victorian England* (London, 1974); D. A. Hamer, *The Politics of Electoral Pressure* (Brighton, 1977); Derek Fraser, *Urban Politics in Victorian England* (London, 1976).

Appendix: Parliament and its procedures

The *House of Lords* consisted of all peers of British or United Kingdom creation. Those peers whose titles were of Scottish creation (i.e. they pre-dated the Act of Union of 1707) or of Irish creation (pre-dating the Act of Union of 1800) did not sit in the House of Lords by automatic right, but elected from among their own number sixteen Scottish and twenty-eight Irish peers who sat as 'Representative peers'. All peerages were hereditary in our period. Twenty-six bishops and archbishops of the Church of England, and four from the Church of Ireland (until 1871), also sat in the Lords, but they did so by virtue of their office and not by personal hereditary right.

The *House of Commons* consisted entirely of elected representatives known as Members of Parliament (MPs). Their numbers varied between 654 and 670 during our period. Until 1911 MPs received no salary. The franchise on which MPs were elected varied according to the constituency, and underwent important reforms in 1832, 1867 and 1884. Sittings of the House of Commons were regulated by the Speaker, who was an MP elected by his fellow members.

In October 1834 the Parliament buildings were badly damaged by fire, and this meant that until 1852 the House of Commons met in the chamber normally used by the House of Lords, while the peers used another chamber.

Parliaments were elected for seven-year terms, but they could be dissolved early by an act of the royal prerogative, undertaken at the prime minister's request.

Parliamentary sessions usually began in February and lasted until July or August. Emergency sessions were occasionally summoned at other times in the year. At the beginning of each session, the King's or Queen's speech outlined the policy of the government. A reply was then made, in the form of an Address to the Crown, which provided the occasion for a general debate.

Bills introduced by the government were known as Public bills. Those initiated by back-bench MPs were known as private members' bills. Much nineteenth-century legislation took the form of private bills, sponsored by outside interests, relating to turnpikes, railways, enclosures of land and so on.

A bill had to pass through several stages in the House of Commons. The first reading was normally a routine matter of introducing the bill, and only in extremely controversial cases might it be challenged by forcing a division. Far more important was the debate on the second reading, when the general principles of the bill were discussed. If the bill survived this stage, it proceeded into committee, where it was scrutinised in detail, clause by clause. Most public and private members' bills were in fact dealt with by the whole House of Commons, sitting as a committee, but they might be referred to a specialist select committee, and this was the standard procedure for private bills. Once the committee stage was complete, the bill was 'reported' back to the House of Commons, and then it was debated again on the third reading. The entire process was repeated in the House of Lords, and only after this could the bill receive the royal assent and become an *Act* of Parliament.

1

Constitution and society in the age of Bagehot

The most celebrated and compelling contemporary account of the working of the political system in Victorian Britain is that provided by the journalist, Walter Bagehot, in his study *The English Constitution*, which originally appeared as a series of articles in the *Fortnightly Review* before being published in book form in 1867.[1] Bagehot's analysis is of profound importance for the way he disposed of the popular orthodoxy of his day, which held that the key to understanding the successful working of Britain's Constitution lay in the separation of powers between the executive (responsible for administering the nation's affairs) and the legislature (Parliament). Instead, Bagehot demonstrated that in practice the executive and legislative functions were fused in the body of the Cabinet, which consisted of ministers who were at the head of the executive, but who were at the same time accountable to Parliament, in which they sat. It was the Cabinet that settled the broad outlines of government policy and then used its organised support in Parliament to push those policies through. By describing how the Constitution *really* worked, as opposed to how it was said to operate by more philosophical observers of the scene, Bagehot made an enduring contribution to the British people's appreciation of their own political system.

It is an extraordinary fact, however, that for a book that was, and is, deservedly influential, so many aspects of the argument it put forward should be highly questionable. One point that is of particular concern to us is Bagehot's use of the concept of 'deference' as a means of explaining why the mass of the British people were attached to their nation's political institutions. This emphasis on 'deference' itself followed from the famous distinction Bagehot made between what he called the 'dignified' and the 'efficient' parts of the Constitution. The monarchy and the House of Lords, it was argued, had been deprived of their political power, but they continued to perform a ceremonial function which was designed to dazzle and impress the masses, who were unable to comprehend that these institutions no longer governed the country. As Bagehot put it, 'The separation of principal power from principal station is a refinement which they [the people] could not even conceive.'[2] Effective political power, according to Bagehot, resided in the Cabinet, the 'efficient' part of the Constitution, which he likened to a board of directors appointed by Parliament. Since the Great Reform Act of 1832, the 'middle classes' had been the dominant political force in the country, or so Bagehot claimed, but this reality had been cleverly concealed from the masses by the careful preservation of the 'dignified' elements of the Constitution, the Crown and the peerage, whose *'theatrical show'* secured the deferential loyalty of the people.[3] In this way, Bagehot concluded, it had been possible to deceive the multitude into accepting a system of government which was controlled, behind the scenes, by the solid, worthy, but unspectacular 'middle classes'.

The immediate objection to Bagehot's analysis is that while the 'middle classes' were undoubtedly a considerable force in the constituencies, and their views were influential in determining government policy, as the repeal of the Corn Laws in 1846 shows, their grip on the levers of political power at Westminster seems to have been remarkably slight. Bagehot identified the Cabinet as the 'efficient secret' of the Constitution, but few men of middle-class origins belonged to it in the 1860s. If we take the Liberal Cabinet formed by Earl Russell in October 1865 (around the time *The English Constitution* was beginning to appear in article form), we find that of the fourteen ministers, eight were peers and two were landed baronets, while of the remainder only Edward Cardwell and W. E. Gladstone could be said to have 'middle class' backgrounds; and Gladstone, as is well known, was the son of a successful merchant who became a landowner and eventually a baronet, and young William was sent to Eton and Oxford, and therefore never worked in 'business'. Similarly with the Conservative Cabinet formed by the Earl of Derby in June 1866, it emerges that of the fifteen members, five were peers, four were the sons of peers, and two were landed baronets. It is difficult to see how anyone in this Cabinet could be meaningfully categorised as 'middle class', except perhaps the lawyer, Spencer Walpole, though he was descended from an Earl on the maternal side. Benjamin Disraeli, the son of a literary man, would certainly not have appreciated the label 'middle class', and in any case he had long since been set up as a landed gentleman by his political friends.

This glaring weakness in Bagehot's argument makes one wonder if he seriously believed in it himself. In fact, his definition of the 'middle classes' turns out to be so vague – he meant by it not simply business and professional people, but all those who were well educated – as to be virtually meaningless. How, by Bagehot's criterion, could his 'middle classes' be distinguished from the traditional ruling elite of aristocrats and landowners, who were likely to be well educated? Such difficulties tend to confirm the suspicion expressed by Richard Crossman, in his 1963 introduction to *The English Constitution*, that the process of constitutional development described by Bagehot was not what *had* happened, but what he felt *ought* to happen.[4] In other words, Bagehot had a hidden agenda: his claim that the middle classes exercised real power through the 'efficient' part of the Constitution, the Cabinet, but obscured this fact from the eyes of the masses by allowing it to appear that the 'dignified' components of the Constitution still ruled, was shaped by his concern to prevent the enfranchisement of large numbers of 'ignorant' working men. Franchise reform was very much in the political air by the mid-1860s, and Bagehot dreaded a measure which he believed would undermine a system of government that had produced years of balanced, moderate rule. The irony of the matter, of course, is that no sooner had *The English Constitution* appeared in book form than Derby's Conservative ministry rudely upset Bagehot's hopes by passing precisely the sort of Reform Act that he had been anxious to see avoided.

If the picture painted by Bagehot of a Constitution cunningly designed by the 'middle classes' in order to secure the deferential allegiance of the masses is, surely, a mythical one, it may be possible to go further and challenge the assertion that the 'dignified' parts of the Constitution, the monarchy and the House of Lords, had been reduced to a purely decorative role.

There can be no doubt that by the 1860s the direct political power exercised by Queen Victoria was considerably less than that of, say, her grandfather, George III (reigned 1760–1820). This situation reflected the fundamental change that had taken place, during the early decades of the nineteenth century, in the way governments were maintained in power, with organised parliamentary parties, rather than the royal prerogative, becoming the essential basis of support. In the 1780s, for example, William Pitt the Younger was not at the head of a large party, but owed his position as Prime Minister to the favour of George III, who had dismissed the preceding Fox-North coalition government. The fact that Pitt was the king's choice as Prime Minister ensured that he received the general support of large numbers of 'independent' MPs who were unattached to political parties, and it also meant that important patronage resources were at his disposal which could be used to secure the support of other politicians. By contrast, when William IV (1830–37) tried to exercise the royal prerogative in a similar way, he met with a humiliating defeat. Although William did dismiss Lord Melbourne's ministry, in November 1834, his alternative Prime Minister, Sir Robert Peel, was unable to sustain his new government because he could not command a majority in the House of Commons. Even the king's use of his prerogative power to grant a dissolution of Parliament, so that a general election could be held, was not enough to rectify the situation, and by April 1835, Peel felt obliged to resign and William was compelled to reinstate Melbourne.

What had changed, between the age of Pitt the Younger and the age of Peel, was partly that the personal prestige of the monarchy had waned, thanks to the unpopularity of George IV (1820–30), but also that a series of Economical Reform bills had diminished the amount of Crown patronage available to the Prime Minister. Most important of all, there was no longer a large body of 'independent' MPs prepared to rally to the support of the king's chosen Minister. The crisis over parliamentary reform in the early 1830s, the consequent creation of a radically altered electoral system in 1832, and the persistence of controversial religious and constitutional issues for the remainder of the decade, all served to polarise the House of Commons into 'Liberal' and 'Conservative' camps, with few MPs lacking a basic party affiliation.[5] William IV's experience thus helped to establish that it was necessary for the monarch to operate within a framework of popular sovereignty, as expressed through the medium of parliamentary parties. This lesson was reinforced when the young Queen Victoria, who succeeded to the throne in 1837, endeavoured, for personal reasons, to keep Melbourne in power between 1839 and 1841, in spite of the fact that by this time his government's majority in the House of Commons had evaporated. Victoria succeeded in the short term, preventing Peel from taking office in 1839 when she refused his request to change some of her ladies of the bedchamber (they were all from good Liberal families), but in the summer of 1841 a general election produced a decisive victory for Peel and the Conservatives, and the queen had no choice but to accept him as Prime Minister.

The ability of the Victorian monarchy to come to terms with these changing circumstances was in large part due to the influence, behind the scenes, of the queen's husband, Prince Albert of Saxe-Coburg-Gotha (they were married in 1840). Under Albert's tutelage, Victoria came to recognise the need for the monarchy to be seen to be above the political fray, independent of any party, by adopting a neutral stance in the exercise of its prerogative powers. However, it is important to note that Albert's vision of a constitutional monarchy was one in which the queen, while avoiding any nakedly partisan use of her constitutional powers, would continue to exert great influence over her ministers, and it was in order to attain this end that Albert, acting as his wife's private secretary, maintained a close supervision over the main areas of government policy. The reality of the Crown's political influence behind the scenes is evidenced by the dismissal of the Foreign Secretary, Palmerston, in December 1851, because of his unwillingness to consult with the Court before forming his policies; and a year later Victoria and Albert were to be active in promoting their pet project of a Liberal/Peelite coalition government, with Lord Aberdeen as Prime Minister. In many ways, it appears as if the decisive event in the development of the modern constitutional monarchy was the premature death of Albert in December 1861, at the age of only 42. Thereafter the widowed Victoria lacked the requisite intellect, stamina and powers of application with which to effectually scrutinise her

9

ministers' actions, though her nuisance value continued to be substantial.[6]

A careful reading of Bagehot's account of the monarchy, in *The English Constitution*, reveals that he was perfectly well aware of the wide scope that still existed for a monarch to influence ministerial policy. This is indicated by his famous formula that the queen possessed 'the right to be consulted, the right to encourage, [and] the right to warn.' It is even stated explicitly, when Bagehot acknowledged that Prince Albert 'really did gain great power' through his energetic and assiduous attention to the detail of government: indeed, Bagehot continued, 'If his life had been prolonged twenty years, his name would have been known to Europe as that of King Leopold [of the Belgians] is known'.[7] The admission that the monarchy in Albert's time had actually increased its power, is clearly in violent contradiction to the claim made by Bagehot, elsewhere in his book, that it was merely a 'dignified' part of the Constitution.

Bagehot's depiction of a 'dignified' monarchy, whose energies were occupied primarily in fulfilling its symbolic functions, is arguably of greater interest as a percipient view of what the institution was increasingly to become, rather than as an accurate account of the situation as it had been in the recent past. Certainly, from the 1870s onwards, the growing consciousness among the British people of their country's status as a great imperial power translated into a growing enthusiasm for the monarchy as a symbol of imperial, as well as national, unity, as is testified by the spectacular Jubilee celebrations of 1887 and 1897.[8] One might even suggest that this phenomenon was one that was imposed upon the queen by her enthusiastic subjects, rather than something she actively sought for herself. But it would be a serious mistake to suppose that the monarchy ever became a hollow shell, in terms of its constitutional powers. For instance, the responsibility for appointing the Prime Minister still rested with the Crown, and while there were occasions when Victoria found her choice circumscribed, as in 1880 when a landslide election victory for the Liberals obliged her to accept the detested Gladstone, in other circumstances she still exercised a real choice. This was particularly true when a new prime ministerial appointment was required *during* the lifetime of a Parliament, since there was no mechanism by which the party in government could elect its own leader. The decision rested with the queen, and her choice of Lord Salisbury rather than Sir Stafford Northcote, in 1885, and of Lord Rosebery rather than Sir William Harcourt, in 1894, were genuine applications of Victoria's prerogative power.

Similar doubts may be felt about the validity of Bagehot's treatment of the other element in the 'dignified' part of the Constitution, the House of Lords. This is not to deny that since the parliamentary reform crisis of 1831–32 the Lords had been thrown back into a defensive position. On that occasion, the Lords' resistance to the Reform bill, introduced by Earl Grey's government, was overcome when ministers prevailed upon King William IV to pledge himself to the creation, if necessary, of a large number of new peers in order to swamp the existing hostile majority. Confronted by a government with a majority in the House of Commons, which was determined to have its way, and which was buttressed in its position by clear evidence of public support for its measure, the House of Lords was obliged to give way and allow the Reform bill to pass. Undoubtedly, this episode was a major psychological blow to the authority and prestige of the Upper House, and it is noticeable that the leader of the Conservative peers, the Duke of Wellington, did his utmost in the years that followed to avoid any further collision with the House of Commons. When, many years later, in 1860–61, another dispute did arise between the two Houses, concerning the repeal of the paper duties, it was again the opinion of the Commons that prevailed, and repeal was carried.[9] Writing about the position of the House of Lords in *The English Constitution*, a few years after the paper duties crisis, Bagehot took the view that the Upper House had been weakened, constitutionally, by the fact that it represented the interests of only one class in society, the landowning aristocracy, and that in consequence it had been relegated to the useful, but not essential, subordinate function of a revising chamber for legislation sent up from the House of Commons.[10]

The obvious objection to Bagehot's argument is that, while the House of Lords had evidently become more cautious about exercising its powers, the fact remained that those powers were unchanged. In theory, at least, the Upper House still possessed an unlimited right to veto legislation, and so long as this was the case the potential existed for future constitutional conflict. Signs of a growing assertiveness on the part of the House of Lords were to become apparent in the years immediately following the publication of *The English Constitution*. Gladstone's Liberal ministry had to force the peers to back down over their drastic amendments to the bill to disestablish and disendow the Irish Church in 1869, and two years later ministers circumvented the Lords' resistance to the Army Regulation bill by resorting to a royal warrant in order to achieve the bill's main objective of abolishing the system whereby army commissions were purchased. (It is ironic, given Bagehot's argument about the monarchy, that in 1871, as in 1832, the royal prerogative had to be invoked in order to override the House of Lords.) On both these occasions the Lords may have been defeated, but they nevertheless indicated that the friction between the two Houses of Parliament was becoming more, not less, intense, and we shall see in chapter 5 how this contributed to the general growth of political partisanship during the later decades of the nineteenth century.

While the constitutional privileges of the House of Lords remained intact, it is also important to bear in mind that, the threatened mass-creation of peers in 1832 having proved unnecessary, the composition of the Upper House was unaltered. Bagehot claimed that this served to weaken the authority of the Lords, but to some extent he undid his own handiwork when he acknowledged, in another chapter of *The English Constitution*, the continued prominence of peers at the highest levels of government. Indeed, he went so far as to describe the House of Lords as a 'reservoir' of Cabinet ministers.[11] If we take the seventy-year period (1830–1900) covered in this book, the premiership itself was held by peers for a total of roughly thirty years, and the Foreign Secretaryship for roughly fifty years. (Neither of these figures, incidentally, takes account of Lord Palmerston, who, as an Irish peer, did not have an automatic right to a seat in the Upper House, and preferred instead to be an MP: his long tenure at the Foreign Office amounted to about sixteen years, and he was subsequently Prime Minister for well over nine years.) At one point during Palmerston's second administration, in 1863, the Foreign Secretary, Colonial Secretary, Secretary of State for War, and First Lord of the Admiralty, were all in the House of Lords.

Returning to Bagehot's central assertion that the British were a deferential people, this appears much too facile, at least in the way Bagehot formulated it, as an explanation for the masses' acceptance of their nation's political institutions. It may well be true, as Bagehot claimed, that a large proportion of the population were too ignorant to appreciate his distinction between the 'dignified' and the 'efficient' parts of the Constitution (even elementary education, after all, did not become compulsory until 1880), but in view of what we have seen about the way the monarchy and the House of Lords did operate, the uninformed masses could perhaps be forgiven for believing that these institutions still wielded much power. The Crown and the aristocracy did not *surrender* their powers, but they came to accept stricter limits on the way those powers were exercised, and it was increasingly recognised that political primacy rested with the elective portion of the Constitution, the House of Commons. It might therefore be suggested that, far from the minds of the masses simply being captivated by the ceremonial display of Crowns and coronets, it was the proven ability of the British Constitution to adapt to meet the requirements and expectations of a rapidly changing society, that earned for it the acceptance of the British public. If there was a deferential relationship between rulers and ruled, this was a two-way process, involving rights and obligations on both sides, rather than a matter of unquestioning acceptance of static constitutional arrangements. This faculty for political adjustment was one that manifested itself in a variety of other ways. For instance, a general reformation of the public manners of the ruling elite seems to have taken place, by the middle of the nineteenth century, under the influence of the 'evangelical revival', which meant that overtly immoral forms of behaviour were no longer tolerated.[12] Moreover, the flexibility of the system was demonstrated by the process, commencing in 1832, by which the parliamentary franchise was gradually extended to embrace important social groups.

When considered from a wider, European perspective, there was good reason for Britons to express a sense of pride in the way their nation's political institutions had evolved. Of the major European powers, Austria, Prussia and Russia were still ruled as autocracies in the early nineteenth century, and the absence of proper representative institutions had resulted in revolutions which threatened the Austrian and Prussian crowns in 1848. As for Britain's western neighbour, France, she had exhibited such a degree of political instability, lurching from monarchy to republic to empire and so on, that she seemed to serve as a warning against any sudden and dramatic experiments in 'democracy'. The key to Britain's stability and success, it was therefore believed, lay in the fact that she had undergone a long-term process of constitutional growth, dating back to the 'Glorious Revolution' of 1688, when arbitrary monarchy had been over-thrown and parliamentary government firmly established. This gratifying sense of the superiority of Britain's Constitution – and by implication also of the superiority of the British 'national character' – was exemplified by the writings and speeches of Thomas Babington Macaulay, who was both a historian, writing a multi-volume *History of England* (1848–54), and a politician who had eloquently defended the Reform bill of 1832. According to the 'Whig' interpretation of history, as expounded by Macaulay in a speech at Edinburgh in 1852, the fact that the revolutionary 'madness of 1848' had not spread to Britain was due to the sagacity of past generations of her statesmen, who had recog-nised the need for timely reform. Consequently, in Britain in 1848:

> we knew that though our Government was not a perfect Govern-ment, it was a good Government, that its faults admitted of peace-able and legal remedies, that it had never inflexibly opposed just demands, that we had obtained concessions of inestimable value, not by beating the drum, not by ringing the tocsin ... but by the mere force of reason and public opinion.[13]

Expressed in a more blatantly chauvinistic form, such senti-ments about Britain's superior constitutional development, com-pared to the rest of Europe, provided Lord Palmerston with a fertile political theme. During his long tenure of the Foreign Office, and later during his two premierships (1855–58, 1859–65), when he made a number of public speeches in the provincial towns, Palmerston encouraged his listeners to believe that Britain, as the outstanding 'Liberal' power in Europe, was acting as the cham-pion of liberty. British foreign policy, he maintained, was ded-icated to the defence of the rights of 'oppressed nationalities', such as the Hungarians, Italians and Poles. 'A nation exercises a potent influence', he declared on one occasion, 'when it is seen to exhibit a bright example of internal order and morality', and it was Britain's 'moral authority' that enabled her to serve as an object lesson to other countries.[14] Interestingly enough, Palmerston's posturing as the scourge of the European autocrats, particularly the Tsar of Russia during the Crimean War of 1854–56, appears to have had a strong appeal to working-class radicals, including former Chartists, in London. Despite his reputation as a lukewarm reformer at home, the Palmerstonian mix of constitutionalism, patriotism and Russophobia, proved to be remarkably potent.[15]

Given both the high reputation enjoyed by the British Parliament and its proven capacity for gradual evolution, as evidenced by the franchise reforms of 1832, 1867 and 1884, it can be argued that no special explanation, of the sort provided by Bagehot, is required for the fact that the working classes, as a whole, seem to have been as much attached to the Constitution as any other group in society. The pattern of working-class activity throughout Victoria's reign was strongly marked by the desire to gain entry into the political system, and to work from within it, rather than by notions of overthrowing it by revolutionary means.[16] There were certainly some desperate elements in the Chartist movement of the late 1830s and 1840s, for example, but the movement's greatest efforts were concentrated into drawing up giant petitions, to be presented to Parliament, calling for action to meet their demands. More importantly, following the Reform Acts of 1867 and 1884, which conceded the parliamentary franchise to large numbers of working men, organisations were set up with the objective of increasing working-class representation in the House of Commons. The Labour Representation League (1869) made only a limited impact, securing the election of two miners, Thomas Burt and Alexander MacDonald, in 1874, before it was absorbed into the ranks of the Liberal Party. However, the Labour Representation Committee (1900) was to prove to be a much more formidable organisation, receiving as it did substantial funding from trade unions, and the election of twenty-nine of its candidates in 1906 marked the birth of the Parliamentary Labour Party. Both of these organisations testify to the fact that the mass of the British people desired only to be allowed a place within the nation's existing constitutional structure.[17]

One phenomenon that is of considerable interest in this respect is the growth during the 1880s and 1890s of debating societies, sometimes calling themselves 'Parliaments', in all the major urban centres. At South Lambeth, in the late 1880s, the Parliament had 150 members at its peak: each member joined a party and 'represented' a constituency, there was a Speaker, a government and an opposition, and various parliamentary forms were adopted, such as the Queen's speech and the private members' night. The vexing contemporary question of Home Rule for Ireland dominated proceedings, but other issues like the abolition of the House of Lords (motion rejected), the reform of local government, compulsory vaccination, and the eight-hour working day, were also debated. As might be expected, the membership of the South Lambeth Parliament was dominated by the 're-spectable' working class, especially the 'black-coated proletariat' of clerks and suchlike, who sought to acquire better political knowledge as a means towards self-improvement. The most significant point of all is that the majority of the South Lambeth members were youths under the age of 21 (the minimum age at which males were eligible for the parliamentary franchise), so that these local Parliaments were providing a form of political apprenticeship for the voters of the future.[18]

A further indication of the authority and prestige enjoyed by Parliament in Victorian times is provided by the public's willingness to address petitions to it expressing a range of opinions on a great variety of subjects. There was a remarkable growth of petitioning in the years after the Great Reform Act: whereas a total of 23,283 petitions were received at Westminster during the period 1828–32, by 1838–42 this had risen to 70,072. The peak period for petitions was 1868–72, immediately after the second Reform Act, when a total of 101,573 were presented, containing an annual average of 3,125,350 signatures.[19] These figures can be seen as a testament to the success of the Reform Acts in securing the commitment of the British people to their parliamentary institutions, since they clearly believed that Parliament could be responsive to their views. Pressure groups were notably active in organising petitions, and Parliament was sometimes flooded with them when a highly contentious issue, such as the abolition of Church rates, was due to be debated.[20]

The period from the 1830s through to the mid-1880s was one

in which the Liberal Party was in the political ascendance, and the dominant Liberal ideology of the time placed particular emphasis upon the virtues of 'parliamentary government'. This involved much more than ensuring an appropriate distribution of political power between the different elements of the Constitution, for it reflected the belief that Parliament had a vital role to play in reinforcing that sense of *British* national identity which had only slowly been superimposed upon older local and regional identities.[21] From this point of view, parliamentary politics was not simply the aggregate of local and regional issues, though of course these often intruded into the proceedings at Westminster, but above all the forum in which the affairs of the nation as a whole were conducted. The essential purpose of Parliament was to reconcile the claims of competing sectional interests, and, in this way, to promote social integration.[22] Such an elevated notion of Parliament's function was encouraged by the Liberals' characteristic faith in the power of rational discussion, and reinforced by the fact that MPs of all parties, drawing on the ideas of Edmund Burke, liked to think of themselves as representatives of the nation, and not as mere delegates of their constituents voting according to instructions. Bagehot, himself a Liberal, also acknowledged the importance of Parliament's representative role: 'The lyrical function of Parliament, if I may use such a phrase, is well done; it pours out in characteristic words the characteristic heart of the nation'.[23]

Bagehot was less sure about the effectiveness of parliamentary debates in guiding public opinion, but this was, nevertheless, a second essential component of the Victorian ideology of 'parliamentary government', and one that was widely espoused by politicians. It is noticeable, for instance, how many of the extra-parliamentary pressure groups, such as those campaigning for the repeal of the Corn Laws, the disestablishment of the Church, and temperance reform, attached special importance to the task of raising their causes in Parliament, as a means of lifting the level of public consciousness. Jacob Bright, the champion of the movement for women's suffrage, thus explained to the House of Commons in April 1873 why he found it expedient to raise a debate on the issue year after year: 'we have taken the best means in our power to instruct the people upon a great public question.

The substance of this debate will be carefully reported in the newspapers ... and therefore we shall secure that, for at least one day in the year there will be a general discussion on a question so deeply affecting the interests and privileges of a large portion of Her Majesty's subjects'.[24] To another radical Liberal MP, and staunch parliamentarian, it had seemed a few years earlier that what was so valuable about parliamentary debates was the way that expert knowledge, from various walks of life, could be pooled together: 'This is the use of a Parliament. We educate each other. All knowledge is brought to account. Arguments are weighed ... Even prejudice has a certain use in checking excess in another direction. The decision is taken in the main by a number of shrewd and silent judges, whose ears are ever open and minds are ever at work'.[25]

It may well be the case that, at a psychological level, the Victorians' sense of pride in their system of parliamentary government was enhanced by the chance rebuilding of what now came to be called the 'Palace of Westminster'. In the autumn of 1834 a fire, started when the incineration of exchequer tally sticks got out of control, engulfed St Stephen's chapel, where the House of Commons had sat, and seriously damaged adjacent buildings. It was not until 1852 that the Commons were able to move into their new chamber, and the interior decoration of the whole Palace took many more years to complete. The end result was that the loss of some rather nondescript and dingy old buildings (the pre-1834 House of Commons chamber had been nicknamed 'the black hole of Calcutta') was compensated for by Charles Barry's magnificent neo-Gothic structure with its famous clock tower. A recent study has emphasised the way that the central theme of the design and interior decoration 'highlighted the role of the Crown-in-Parliament'.[26] The House of Lords, where the monarch performed the ceremony of opening Parliament, was lavishly decorated, with wall frescoes of medieval royalty, stained glass windows, and an imposing throne, and the royalist theme was likewise applied to the Commons chamber. To an innocent observer, the impression might easily have been given that the authority of the Crown was greater than ever. Surprisingly, Bagehot made no reference in his book to the new Palace of Westminster, but the rich ornamentation, inside and outside, and the implicit emphasis on Parliament's ceremonial aspect, serve to demonstrate just how artificial was Bagehot's distinction between the 'dignified' and the 'efficient' parts of the Constitution.

******

Bagehot's object in writing *The English Constitution*, as we suggested earlier, was to highlight the virtues of a political system in which power allegedly rested with the educated classes. To his horror, however, in the same year that his book was published, the politicians chose to ignore his warning about the dangers of admitting the untutored masses into the Constitution, and proceeded down the 'democratic' path by introducing household suffrage for the boroughs. Seventeen years later, a similar measure was passed for the counties, with the result that something like 60 per cent of adult males in the United Kingdom were able to register to vote. The remainder of this chapter is concerned with the question of how the politicians, whose natural base for operations was Westminster, responded to the dangers, and opportunities, arising from their own creation of a wider electorate. It is possible to detect changes in the way parliamentarians sought to project themselves into the national imagination, from the 1850s onwards, and these became increasingly relevant after the second Reform Act of 1867. Perhaps equally important, though, was that large numbers of ordinary citizens were seeking to identify themselves with the national political leaders.

Any discussion of the methods employed by Westminster politicians in their endeavours to establish a relationship with the electorate, must be set in the context of the emergence of a relatively sophisticated urban and industrial society. The challenge facing the politicians, in other words, was not merely that there was an increasing number of voters to deal with, but that that increase was occurring because of the need to contain, politically, a society that was experiencing rapid and profound change. It was during the Victorian era that the cumulative effects of the processes collectively known as the 'Industrial Revolution' really made themselves felt. The population was growing at a rate in excess of 10 per cent, in each decade of the nineteenth century, so that whereas in 1831 there were 16.37 million people in Britain, by 1901 the figure had reached 37 million.[27] In 1831, the majority of the population still lived in rural areas, but by 1861 the relentless growth of industry, trade, finance and other sectors of the economy, meant that town dwellers outnumbered the rural population for the first time. By 1901, three-quarters of the population of England and Wales lived in towns, and one-third of the total lived in large towns of over 100,000 people. In addition to the geographical concentration of population, the country was being brought closer together, in terms of time, as a result of the revolution in communications associated with the development of the world's first railway network. As early as 1850, 6,084 miles of track had been laid down and 54.4 million passengers were being carried, and by 1900 the corresponding figures were 18,680 miles of track and 1,114.6 million passengers. The spread of the railway network also facilitated the development of a telegraph system, which enabled messages to be transmitted swiftly from one part of the country to another. By the end of the century, motor cars and telephones were just beginning to make an impact, and their effect was to speed up communications still further, and to tailor them more closely to the needs of individuals. Generally speaking, the second half of the nineteenth century saw substantial improvements in living standards for the majority of workers, and this was especially true of the last quarter of the century, when people benefited as consumers from the falling price of many foodstuffs. Indeed, this period witnessed the creation of a mass consumer society, as Britain entered the age of the chain store, of processed foods, of advertising, and so on. In sum, whereas in 1830 Britain, for all its industrial development, in vital respects still resembled a pre-industrial society, with agriculture as its largest industry, by 1900 she had become a recognisably 'modern' society, in the physical sense that her people were predominantly urbanised, and engaged in non-agricultural occupations.

One of the most remarkable features of our period was the enormous expansion of the newspaper industry, as a proliferation of titles occurred both in London and the rest of the country. The growth of the press was in itself very much a product of the industrial and urban age, facilitated as it was by new technology such as steam-powered printing machines, and by the railway and telegraphic communications. Incidentally, the Telegraph Act of 1868, by providing favourable rates for newspapers, finally enabled the provincial press to catch up with their London counterparts, chronologically speaking, so that they were no longer a day behind in reporting news from the metropolis. Improving living standards, and the spread of elementary education, also helped to create a dynamic market for printed news, and governments made their contribution by helping to lower the price of newspapers, through the abolition of the stamp duty in 1855, and of the duty on paper in 1861. The following table provides a clear picture of the consequent expansion of newspaper titles, including dailies and weeklies:[28]

Table 1.1 *Growth in the numbers of British newspapers*

Year	London	Provinces	Wales	Scotland
1824	31	135	?	58
1856	154	375	18	118
1871	261	851	53	131
1886	409	1,225	83	193

Newspapers and periodicals were clearly important, so far as the publicising of politics was concerned, because of the extensive coverage they often provided of proceedings in Parliament. Events at Westminster, and the personalities involved in them, were also brought to life for the ordinary reading public through the work of the parliamentary sketchwriters, whose craft had its origins in the 1850s. One of the earliest notable practitioners was, interestingly enough, the doorkeeper of the House of Commons, William White, who wrote a regular column for the weekly *Illustrated Times*, entitled 'The Inner Life of the House of Commons'. A similar column appeared in the rival *Illustrated London News*, and the format was imitated by many of the provincial papers. The most famous of all the Victorian parliamentary sketchwriters was Henry Lucy, who started work for the *Daily News* in 1872, and in 1881 became *Punch's* 'Toby MP', writing its 'Essence of Parliament' feature. Significantly, both White and Lucy were radical-Liberals in their own politics, but the tone of their articles, while far from uncritical, was usually affectionate and even indulgent, contrasting sharply with the pungent coverage provided by E. M. Whitty in the column he wrote for *The Leader*, a London weekly, in the early 1850s. Perhaps another sign of the way that the treatment of politicians was becoming more mannered, was the appearance in the 1850s of the first political gossip column, 'The Lounger in the Clubs' (Edmund Yeats), in the *Illustrated Times*. At about the same time, the satirical magazine *Punch* (established in 1841) was losing much of the crudeness and savagery which had characterised the cartoons of previous generations, and the works of the great cartoonists of the last decades of the century, like Harry Furniss and Linley Sambourne, were playfully irreverent. From the pen of John Tenniel, indeed, politicians were likely to be depicted as heroic figures from Greek mythology – though the quality of the humour was none the less effective for that.

As the nineteenth century drew to a close, newspapers were giving rather less coverage than before to parliamentary proceedings, but this was compensated for by the growing interest in politicians' public speeches. It has recently been shown that Lord Palmerston was the first politician of the front rank to recognise the potential advantages of provincial speaking tours, the most notable of which he conducted at critical moments in his governments' fortunes, in 1856 and 1864. Palmerston demonstrated a shrewd sense of how to flatter his audiences' civic pride, and so approachable was he that he even encouraged deputations from working men's groups, which he was usually able to win over with his personal charm.[29] W. E. Gladstone, who exploited public speechmaking as a means towards establishing his position as Palmerston's successor, in the early 1860s, seems to have learned more from the veteran leader than he would ever have cared to admit. Disraeli was never naturally at home on the public platform, unlike his great rival, and his appearances were therefore much less common, but his famous speeches at Manchester and the Crystal Palace, in 1872, which helped to consolidate his position as Conservative leader at a time when it was being questioned, were outstanding exceptions to the rule. The classic manifestation of 'stumping' came, of course, with Gladstone's Midlothian campaigns of 1879–80, when he launched a systematic public assault on the policies of Disraeli's (now Earl of Beaconsfield's) government. Gladstone was able to do this in spite of the fact that Midlothian was a small county constituency, where traditional forms of landlord influence were still strong on both sides, because the developments in newspaper technology and telegraphic communications mentioned earlier, meant that he was in reality addressing the country as a whole. People could read each of Gladstone's speeches in their newspapers the morning after he made them. An atmosphere of excitement was thus generated, as Gladstone's speaking tour made its progress through the constituency.[30] Less often remembered is the frequency with which Disraeli's successor as Conservative leader, Lord Salisbury, appeared on public platforms during the last decades of the century. He made no less than seventy speeches in the 1880–85 period, and enjoyed considerable success with his lucid, direct, hard-hitting style, even though he could never hope to match the melodrama of a Gladstonian oration.[31]

It is not an exaggeration to describe Gladstone and Disraeli as cult figures, by the 1870s and 1880s, in terms of their public personalities. In an age of mass-production this even took the form of the sale of memorabilia, such as portraits, busts, plates and mugs, depicting the political heroes. (Conversely, a chamberpot intended for Conservative use had a picture of Gladstone on the inside!) Cheap railway travel meant that people from the northern towns could go on excursions to Gladstone's home, Hawarden Castle in North Wales, to see the great man indulge in his favourite pastime of felling trees, and collect the wood-chips as souvenirs. Interestingly, the cult of Disraeli was substantially a posthumous phenomenon, promoted by the Primrose League, founded in his memory in 1883. The declared aim of the League was 'the maintenance of Religion, of the Estates of the Realm, and of the unity of the British Empire under our Sovereign'. Here, if anywhere, we can detect a politics of deference. The Primrose League, like the rebuilt Palace of Westminster, was a manifestation of the Victorian cult of medievalism: local 'habitations' were given a hierarchical structure, with knights, esquires, dames and so on, and they were linked to district organisations with Saxon names like Northumbria and Mercia, while at the centre there was a Grand Council headed by the Grand Master – an office held by senior Conservative politicians, including Salisbury, Northcote and Balfour. Primrose League habitations offered a regular programme of social events, such as dances, teas, fêtes, excursions, and outings for cycling groups, and the political message was slipped in subtly through short speeches or lantern shows. The Primrose League established a fairly comprehensive network throughout England and Wales, and it became *the* mass political organisation of the late nineteenth century. Its membership reached one million in 1891, and two million by 1910, half of whom were female (women were most useful as canvassers at election time, although they could not vote themselves), and socially it spanned the working and lower-middle classes.[32] Politics and leisure were thus inextricably linked together, with ordinary people being encouraged to participate, albeit vicariously, in the national political life of Britain.

At a less refined level, it can be suggested that the music hall, a predominantly working-class form of entertainment from the 1860s onwards, performed a similar function. Music hall songs of this period were characterised by an increased reverence for the monarchy, enthusiasm for the empire (seen as a field of opportunity for working people), and blatant xenophobia. The notorious chorus to a song composed in 1877: 'We don't want to fight, but by jingo if we do / We've got the ships, we've got the men, and got the money too', was directed against Russia, whose advance towards Constantinople (Istanbul) was perceived as a threat to Britain's land route to her prized imperial possession, India. In spite of these expressions of intense national pride, a vulgar scepticism about the motives and morality of individual politicians was exhibited, and a lurid pleasure taken in the divorce scandals which destroyed the careers of Sir Charles Dilke and Charles Stewart Parnell. The Liberal leader, Gladstone, became a frequent target of quite virulent attacks – the refrain of one song began: 'W. E. G.'s in a state of lunacy' – but a sneaking admiration for the 'craftiness' of Disraeli was often apparent:[33]

Great Dizzie, our Premier, knows well his book,
He's as tricky as here and there one,
When he purchased the Suez canal we all thought
It the very best thing he had done.
Since then of our Queen he's an Empress made,
And however the public may jeer,
He's got his reward, for the Queen in return
As Earl Beaconsfield made him a peer.

More soberly, the extension of the borough franchise in 1867 to include large numbers of working men, prompted the founding, under the auspices of local middle-class politicians, of political clubs aiming to encourage self-education, especially amongst the young. In the industrial towns of South Lancashire, where these clubs have been studied, it appears that large memberships were attracted: lectures, debates and library facilities were arranged, but these were typically combined with various forms of social entertainment like dances, picnics, and the provision of billiards tables. These clubs have been described as 'agents of political socialisation',[34] meaning that they helped to assimilate the newly-enfranchised working classes into the values and practices of the existing political culture of Britain.

******

The closer integration of parliamentary politics and society in Victorian Britain can be seen as a success story, helping to secure an impressive degree of political stability, but at the same time revitalising the political system through the absorption of millions of new voters. This achievement was not without certain costs, however, in terms of the growth of overt political partisanship, both at Westminster and in the country, which seemed necessary in order to sustain the attention and enthusiasm of the public. A populist style of politics inevitably came into conflict with the collusive tactics often employed by the Westminster elite in an effort to minimise the effects of party strife. The aim in the remainder of this book is to trace the ways in which the conduct of politics at the parliamentary level changed in response to the pressures and expectations generated by the emergence of a wider political audience.

Notes

1 Walter Bagehot, *The English Constitution*, ed. R. H. S. Crossman (London, 1963). Bagehot was being deplorably anglocentric, of course, in referring to the English rather than the British Constitution.

2 *Ibid.*, p. 241.

3 *Ibid.*, p. 248.

4 *Ibid.*, pp. 26–9.

5 David Close, 'The Formation of a Two-Party Alignment in the House of Commons between 1832 and 1841', *English Historical Review*, LXXXIV (1969), pp. 257–77.

6 David Cannadine, 'The Last Hanoverian Monarch? The Victorian Monarchy in Historical Perspective', in A. L. Beier *et al.* (eds.), *The First Modern Society* (London, 1989), pp. 127–66.

7 *English Constitution*, pp. 111–13. King Leopold of the Belgians (died 1865) was uncle to both Victoria and Albert, and the main influence on Albert's constitutional thinking.

8 David Cannadine, 'The Context, Performance and meaning of ritual: the British Monarchy and "the invention of tradition" ', in E. J. Hobsbawm and T. Ranger (eds.), *The Invention of Tradition* (Cambridge, 1983), pp. 101–64.

9 G. H. L. Le May, *The Victorian Constitution* (London, 1979), pp. 132–3.

10 *English Constitution*, pp. 128–34. E. A. Wasson's recent article, 'The Crisis of the Aristocracy: Parliamentary Reform, the Peerage and the House of Commons, 1750–1914', *Parliamentary History*, XIII (1994), pp. 297–311, emphasises the way that the 1832 Reform Act weakened the peers' control over elections to the Commons. It might be noted, though, that the table on p. 305 of noblemen MPs is arguably distorted by the rapid expansion of the peerage in the early decades of the 19th century. In fact, Wasson's figure for 1860 (25.2 per cent) is only slightly lower than that for 1801 (27.9 per cent).

11 *English Constitution*, p. 67.

12 David Spring, 'Aristocracy, Social Structure, and Religion in the early Victorian Period', *Victorian Studies*, VI (1963), pp. 263–80.

13 H. J. Hanham (ed.), *The Nineteenth Century Constitution* (Cambridge, 1969), pp. 12–13.

14 E. D. Steele, *Palmerston and Liberalism, 1855–1865* (Cambridge, 1991), p. 26.

15 Anthony Taylor, 'Palmerston and Radicalism, 1847–1865', *Journal of British Studies*, XXXIII (1994), pp. 157–79.

16 The outright repudiation of Parliament was always a minority strand within popular radical thinking: T. M. Parssinen, 'Association, Convention and Anti-Parliament in British Radical Politics, 1771–1848', *English Historical Review*, LXXXVIII (1973), pp. 504–33.

17 The same argument can be applied, of course, to the suffragette campaign of the Edwardian period.

18 John W. Davis, 'Working Class Make Believe: The South Lambeth Parliament (1887–1890)', *Parliamentary History*, XII (1993), pp. 249–58.

19 Jonathan Parry, *The Rise and Fall of Liberal Government in Victorian Britain* (Yale, 1993), pp. 63, 141, 223.

20 T. A. Jenkins (ed.), *The Parliamentary Diaries of Sir John Trelawny, 1858–1865* (Royal Historical Society, Camden Fourth Series, vol. 40, 1990), 25 January, 8 February and 28 March 1860.

21 Linda Colley, *Britons: Forging the Nation, 1707–1837* (Yale, 1992), especially pp. 50–2, 163.

22 Parry, *Rise and Fall of Liberal Government*, pp. 7–14.

23 *English Constitution*, p. 177.

24 Cited by Brian Harrison, *Peaceable Kingdom* (Oxford, 1982), p. 384.

25 *Trelawny Diaries*, 12 March 1863.

26 Roland Quinault, 'Westminster and the Victorian Constitution', *Transactions of the Royal Historical Society*, Sixth Series, II (1992), pp. 79–104.

27 All the figures in this paragraph are from B. R. Mitchell and Phyllis Deane, *Abstract of British Historical Statistics* (Cambridge, 1971).

28 Figures from John Vincent, *The Formation of the British Liberal Party, 1857–68* (London, 1972 edn.), p. 101.

29 Steele, *Palmerston and Liberalism*, pp. 23–42; Taylor, 'Palmerston and Radicalism', pp. 176–9.

30 H. C. G. Matthew (ed.), *The Gladstone Diaries*, IX (Oxford, 1986), pp. lviii-lxix.

31 Lady Gwendolen Cecil, *Life of Robert, Marquis of Salisbury*, 4 vols (London, 1921–32), iii, pp. 63–9.

32 Martin Pugh, *The Tories and the People, 1880–1935* (Oxford, 1985).

33 Laurence Senelick, 'Politics as Entertainment: Victorian Music Hall Songs', *Victorian Studies*, XIX (1975), pp. 149–80.

34 John Garrard, 'Parties, Members and Voters after 1867', in T. R. Gourvish and Alan O'Day (eds.), *Later Victorian Britain 1867–1900* (London, 1988), p. 149.

2

Government, opposition and the party system, 1832–1867

In the field of British parliamentary politics, the period between the first and second Reform Acts has proved to be a conceptually difficult one which continues to envelop itself in an air of confusion. Historians have commonly taken the view that the 1830s witnessed the emergence of a 'modern' two-party system, one in which a well-regimented party of government was confronted by an equally well-organised party of opposition seeking to take its place. This process was associated with two developments mentioned briefly in the last chapter, the decline in the direct power of the Crown, and the virtual disappearance of 'independent' MPs whose first allegiance was to the king's ministers, whoever they might be. However, the picture is complicated by the subsequent crisis and schism in the Conservative Party, resulting from the repeal of the Corn Laws in 1846, and the apparent chaos into which the party system was thrown for the next twenty years. The mid-Victorian period has therefore come to be seen as one in which parties were in decline. Political instability during the 1850s was such that governments resigned on no less than six occasions after suffering defeats in the House of Commons,[1] and the future Liberal leader, W. E. Gladstone, published an article in the *Quarterly Review* in 1856, lamenting what he termed 'The Declining Efficiency of Parliament', which he attributed to the weakness of ministries. Given this sharp contrast between the periods before and after 1846, it has been found necessary to resort to the explanation that the two-party system of the 1830s was an exceptional development, which soon broke down, and was not to be fully restored until after the 1867 Reform Act, when it became a permanently established feature of parliamentary politics.[2]

It should be stressed at once that the basic validity of the first part of the analysis just described, namely the existence by the end of the 1830s of a fairly clear-cut two-party alignment in the House of Commons, is not in serious doubt. For instance, David Close's study of House of Commons division lists, for the Parliament of 1835–37, shows an extremely high level of consistency in the way MPs voted in crucial divisions involving either an overt trial of strength between government and opposition, such as the election of a Speaker or an amendment to the Address, or else major policy issues on which the government had taken a clear stand, such as the abolition of church rates. Using fourteen lists relating to important divisions of this kind, and examining the behaviour of 594 MPs who sat throughout the Parliament's duration, it was found that 259 members voted consistently on the Conservative side and 274 on the Liberal side (though of course they did not all vote in every division), while a further 34 voted consistently with one or other of the parties except on one issue. Only 24 MPs could reasonably be classed as 'independents', in the sense that their voting behaviour indicated no strong commitment to either party, and three others voted too infrequently to make any classification possible. The resulting impression of a House of Commons in which few MPs displayed a genuine lack of allegiance to any political party, also applies to the Parliament of 1837–41, and is confirmed by the work of other scholars.[3]

Recent research has suggested, however, that 'bloc voting', where the overwhelming majority of MPs followed the line taken by their party leaders, with very few wavering, was confined to a limited range of parliamentary divisions. Party loyalty was demonstrated most clearly on precisely those occasions singled out by Close, when the survival or demise of a ministry was seen to depend on the outcome of a vote. In such circumstances, most MPs, whether they were supporters or opponents of the government, had a clear conception of where their duty lay. Thus the newly-elected MP for Leeds, Edward Baines, who supported various radical causes such as the reduction of the armed forces and the repeal of the Corn Laws, defined his relationship with Lord Grey's ministry, in March 1834, as follows: 'I shall vote for each measure upon what I think its merits, unless the Ministers should seem to be at any time in danger, and then I would make some sacrifice of my individual views to serve or to save them'.[4] As Baines's letter suggests, large numbers of parliamentary divisions involved issues which, though of political significance, were not perceived as life-threatening to the government, and here we find a sharp drop in levels of party voting. Ian Newbould has shown, using thirty-eight divisions on major policy issues during the Parliament of 1835–37, that only one-fifth of Liberal MPs voted consistently with Lord Melbourne's government, while two-fifths opposed their own government on up to 10 per cent of the divisions, and a further two-fifths opposed the government *more* than 10 per cent of the time.[5]

The relationship between the Conservative administration of Sir Robert Peel and its House of Commons followers, in the years from 1841 to 1846, bears out the view that demonstrations of back-bench independence were a regular feature of parliamentary politics, but that such conduct was not considered incompatible with a fundamental loyalty to the party leader. During the 1842 session, for example, thirty-two Conservative MPs opposed the government's Poor Law renewal bill, while eighty-five voted against their own Prime Minister in supporting a protectionist motion regarding the cattle duties; in 1843, sixty-five Conservatives opposed the second reading of the Ecclesiastical Courts bill, and in 1844 as many as 106 opposed the second reading of the Dissenters' Chapels bill. In many cases, the votes of MPs reflected constituency pressures in favour of the maintenance of agricultural protection and the defence of the Church of England, and, with the exception of a small number of malcontents, they were not regarded as expressions of a desire to bring down Peel's government. It is in this context that we should assess the two more famous Conservative revolts against Peel's policies, during the 1844 session, which involved opposition to lowering the sugar duties, and support for the bill to fix a ten-hour working day in textile factories. On these issues the government suffered defeats, but Peel's reaction was to confront his own rebels by threatening to resign unless the hostile votes were reversed. In both cases, it became clear that the vast majority of Conservatives were not prepared to persist in a course of action which might lead to the destruction of Peel's government and its probable replacement by a Liberal regime sure to be more hostile to those Anglican and landed interests which the Conservatives were so anxious to preserve. It would be a misunderstanding of the nature of parliamentary politics, therefore, to conclude that the events of 1844 proved that Peel had lost command over his party, and that this foreshadowed an inevitable schism in 1846. Only in the summer of 1845, when controversy raged over Peel's proposal to increase the grant to the Roman Catholic seminary at Maynooth, did many Conservatives become so alienated from their leader that the conditions were created that led ultimately to the fatal rupture over the Corn Law question, the following year.[6]

It should be evident by now that the modern concept of a two-party system, involving rigidly-demarcated parties of government and opposition, is only partially applicable to the period between the first and second Reform Acts.[7] Further demonstration of this point can be provided by reference to the work of Hugh Berrington, who has analysed those House of Commons divisions in which the government whips acted as tellers – an indication that the government had a view on the issues concerned and was trying to direct MPs as to how they should vote. In the following table, 'True two-party votes' are defined as those in which at least 90 per cent of members of both parties voted in accordance with their leaders' wishes; 'Cross-bench votes' are those where moderate MPs of one party voted with the other party in defiance of their own leaders, and 'Extremist votes' are those in which a group of MPs – typically the radical Liberals, who often pressed issues that were of concern to them – were opposed by a majority of *both* parties.[8]

Table 2.1   *Voting behaviour in the House of Commons*

Year	Total whip divisions	True two-party votes (%)	Cross-bench votes (%)	Extremist votes (%)
1836	88	34	33	33
1850	221	18	42	41
1860	173	5	46	50

As Berrington's figures show, straightforward votes dividing the House of Commons along party lines account for scarcely more than one-third of 'whip divisions' in the mid-1830s, when a strong two-party alignment is thought to have been developing, and the figure fell dramatically in the middle decades of the nineteenth century (for reasons we shall discuss shortly). Cross-bench and Extremist voting were almost as prevalent as two-party voting in 1836, and they subsequently overtook it. Of particular interest to us are the figures regarding Extremist voting, for what they mean is that on a large number of whip divisions – exactly half, by 1860 – the leaderships of the two parties were acting together in order to help resist radical proposals emanating either from the 'left' or the 'right' of the political spectrum. The best known example of this strategy comes from the 1830s, when Peel was leader of the opposition: he frequently came to the rescue of Melbourne's government by helping it to vote down radical plans for further parliamentary reform, the repeal of the Corn Laws and so on.[9] But it is important to remember that this was not a unique case, and that Peel himself, as Prime Minister from 1841–46, often received reciprocal support from the opposition, such as on the third reading of the Dissenters' Chapels bill in June 1844, which only passed thanks to Liberal votes (see Doc. 15). Indeed, opposition support was to be vital to the passage of the Maynooth grant and the repeal of the Corn Laws, both of which were bitterly resisted by many back-bench Conservatives. Front-bench collaboration was to remain a normal part of parliamentary voting behaviour until the 1880s: as late as 1883, for example, the party leaderships voted on the same side in 46 per cent of 'whip divisions'.[10]

Once it is accepted that the unquestionable two-party alignment of the 1830s and early 1840s only ever functioned very loosely, and that an MP's allegiance to a party leader did not imply that he could be expected to toe the party line on all occasions, it may be possible for us to dispense with the notion that the party system entered into a period of decline after the Corn Law crisis of 1846. The whole concept of a decline of party, as we noted earlier, was only necessitated by the assumption that prior to 1846 party discipline was strictly enforced, a view that we now see is misleading. It can therefore be suggested that, in terms of MPs party loyalties, there was an underlying continuity throughout the 1832–67 period, no matter how confused the system of parliamentary politics may have appeared after 1846.

Confusion is certainly an apt way of characterising the politics of the 1850s. The key to the instability of this decade is to be found in the rivalry and friction between the individuals and groups who were collectively known as 'Liberals', on the basis of their common commitment to the policy of Free Trade.[11] Competition for the leadership of Liberalism, involving Lord John Russell and Lord Palmerston, was seriously damaging to Liberal unity, which tended to be precarious enough in any case because there were a number of radicals who could never be counted as reliable supporters of any Liberal government. An added dimension to the situation was provided by the uncertain relationship between the Liberals and the Peelites, the latter group consisting of those Conservatives who had broken with their party by supporting the repeal of the Corn Laws in 1846, and who continued to operate independently even after Peel's death in 1850. With such political diversity, it is easy to see why the non-Conservative forces, who constituted a numerical majority of the House of Commons throughout the 1850s, found it so difficult to establish a stable and durable administration. In February 1852, for example, Palmerston and the Peelites were instrumental in the destruction of Russell's ministry; in January 1855 an unhappy experiment in coalition government between Liberals and Peelites collapsed in acrimonious circumstances; while in March 1857 and again in February 1858, Russell, the Peelites and many radicals combined to humiliate Palmerston's government. It was not until June 1859 that a reconciliation took place, and all the non-Conservatives agreed to support a new ministry headed by Palmerston. Even after this, Palmerston's notorious strategy of adopting a very moderate approach to questions of domestic reform ensured that a substantial amount of cross-party voting continued to take place, in spite of the appearance of greater Liberal unity. This helps to account for Berrington's finding, mentioned earlier, that in the 1860 session of Parliament only 5 per cent of 'whip divisions' produced a straight two-party vote, while in 50 per cent of cases the Liberal and Conservative front benches were voting together in order to counter 'extremist dissidence', coming mainly from the radicals. Consistent support for a Liberal government by Liberal MPs, in other words, was still far from being the normal state of affairs.

Some interesting examples of the curious voting patterns that could arise, during the second Palmerston administration of 1859–65, may be found in the reports by the Liberal chief whip, Henry Brand, to the Chancellor of the Exchequer, W. E. Gladstone.

In May 1860, on a division on the budget, Brand found that '46 of the opposition voted with us . . . and 40 of our supporters voted with the opposition'; and in July 1863, when the government was defeated on a Liberal back-bencher's resolution in favour of abolishing the tax on fire insurance policies, Brand's analysis showed that Liberals were in a majority both for and against the proposal, as so many Conservatives were absent:[12]

Voted for Govern		Against	
Libs	51	Libs	54
Cons	18	Cons	49
	69	Irish Ind	
		Opposition	2
			105

Nevertheless, there is considerable evidence to support the view that fundamental party loyalties remained intact, and were readily manifested when occasion required it, even if it is true that those occasions arose less frequently than in the pre-1846 period. Studies of the Conservative Party in the 1850s and early 1860s have demonstrated that it was capable of producing impressive displays of unity on issues of first-class importance, such as the censure motions of June 1855 and March 1857, while on the Liberal side the diary of Sir John Trelawny shows that MPs had a clear perception of whether or not a parliamentary division involved a 'party question' – and apparently 'factious' attacks by the opposition usually prompted the Liberals to rally to their leaders' support.[13] The best indications of the strength of party allegiances are provided by the great divisions on the Liberal motion of 'no confidence' in Derby's government in June 1859, which was carried by 323 votes to 310 (in a House of 658 members), and on the Conservatives' censure motion against Liberal foreign policy in July 1864, which was repelled by 313 votes to 295. Both can be described as straightforward party divisions, in which no more than a handful of MPs on each side declined to follow their leaders, and a comparison of how MPs voted on the two issues together indicates an extremely high level of consistency: a total of twenty-four MPs had switched sides, but ten of these were Irish Roman Catholics who had deserted the Liberal Party because of its support for the Italian Risorgimento, which weakened the temporal power of the Pope.[14] Further proof of the survival of party ties exists in the form of a list of MPs receiving circulars from the whips, compiled by the Conservative chief whip in 1861, showing that only seven members were judged to be 'independents', and these were all maverick radicals of the J. A. Roebuck variety.[15] Interestingly enough, a recent study of the House of Lords has confirmed the strength and sophistication of party management among the peers as well, in the years between 1846 and 1865 when, according to the old interpretation, parties were in decline.[16]

******

Thus far, we have concentrated on the practical evidence of MPs' voting behaviour as a means of ascertaining contemporary attitudes towards party, but such attitudes were naturally reflected in, and influenced by, the constitutional theory of the day. For most of the period covered in this chapter, a tension existed between two competing constitutional nostrums, 'Executive government' and 'Parliamentary government', both of which in fact militated against the acceptance of a rigid two-party structure. According to the concept of 'Executive government', ministers were primarily regarded as servants of the Crown, rather than as party leaders whose first responsibility was to satisfy the wishes of their followers, no matter how much those followers had done to place the ministers in power. After the accession of Queen Victoria in 1837, the Liberal Prime Minister, Lord Melbourne, exhibited a marked inclination towards an 'executive' view of his position, believing as he did that his chief task was to instruct the young monarch in her constitutional duties.[17] The classic exponent of this approach to government, however, was the man who replaced Melbourne as Prime Minister after the Conservatives' election victory in 1841, Sir Robert Peel. Shortly after taking office, Peel informed the House of Commons that he would 'not hold office by the servile tenure which would compel me to be the instrument of carrying other men's opinions into effect', and that, as far as he was concerned, Conservative MPs 'confer on me no personal obligation in having placed me in this office'.[18] It was Peel's determination, as the queen's minister, to conduct government policy in line with what he considered to be the national interest, as instanced by his Free Trade measures and the Maynooth grant, which brought him into conflict with the prejudices of a Conservative Party representing agrarian and Anglican interests, and eventually led to his downfall in 1846. Peel's philosophy of government naturally endeared him to Victoria and Prince Albert, who came to admire what they regarded as a model version of disinterested Statesmanship, rising above the sordid temptations of party self-interest. After Peel's tragic death in 1850, the royal couple were active behind the scenes in seeking to preserve his tradition of 'national government' by promoting a combination between the Peelites and the Liberals, a project which briefly came to fruition with the formation of Lord Aberdeen's coalition government in December 1852. However, this was to be the last occasion when the Crown was able to intervene decisively in ministry-making, before the death of Albert in December 1861, which deprived the queen of her most influential adviser.[19]

While it therefore appears to be the case that by the 1860s commitment to the idea of 'Executive government' was on the wane, the alternative constitutional theory, emphasising the central importance of 'Parliamentary government', enjoyed a continuing vogue.[20] 'Parliamentary government', which was the generally accepted creed of the Liberals by mid-century, found a champion in Walter Bagehot's *The English Constitution* (1867), where it was asserted that the primary function of the House of Commons was not to pass legislation, but to make and unmake governments. 'The House of Commons', Bagehot declared, 'is an electoral chamber; it is the assembly which chooses our President.'[21] What Bagehot meant was that owing to the shift in the balance of constitutional power away from the Crown and towards Parliament, and more specifically towards the House of Commons, the fate of a ministry now depended first and foremost on its standing with the elected chamber. After all, the six Parliaments elected between 1841 and 1865 each brought down at least one government, and in some cases two. In this way, so the Liberal theory of the Constitution ran, Parliament had successfully restricted the prerogative power of the Crown, which in the past had led to arbitrary government. The functioning of political parties was clearly essential to the healthy working of a system of 'Parliamentary government', but the vital point, emphasised for example by the third Earl Grey (the son of the deceased Prime Minister) in his *Parliamentary Government Considered with Reference to Reform of Parliament* (1858), was that these parties were not rigidly organised. A certain amount of fluidity in the party system was considered desirable by Grey, because it helped to ensure that political sovereignty was not transferred directly to the people. This would be the inevitable outcome if parties were so strictly disciplined that the only event that could bring about a change of government was a general election: the electorate, in such a case, was effectively choosing the government by itself. But in a loosely organised two-party system of the sort that existed in Britain between the first and second Reform Acts, in which ministers could never rest upon a solid rock of unquestioning obedience from MPs, Parliament was able to reserve for itself the responsibility of installing and removing governments. 'Parliamentary government' thus acted as a vital check both upon the arbitrary use of royal power, and, equally importantly, upon the potentially despotic power of the people.

******

To summarise the argument which has been developed so far, the early and mid-Victorian party system operated in a way that was sufficiently flexible to ensure that party leaders could never presume upon the support of their back-benchers, who jealously preserved for themselves a degree of latitude, or 'independence', in their political conduct. Allowing for the limits to MPs' party allegiance, however, it remains the case that such allegiances always existed, and even survived the disruption caused by the Corn Law crisis of 1846. It is possible, in other words, to detect an underlying continuity in the party system throughout the period from 1832 to 1867, provided we do not expect too much from this party system and avoid the hazardous temptation of judging it by twentieth-century standards of political behaviour.

There are in fact strong grounds for arguing that, in certain crucial respects, governments were gradually acquiring greater control over Parliament during the period with which we are concerned. One simple reason for this development is that whereas prior to 1832 the function of governments was primarily seen as being executive – the conduct of foreign policy, the defence of the realm and so on – rather than legislative, so that even bills dealing with aspects of social policy were often initiated by back-bench MPs, after the Great Reform Act there was

an increasing expectation that governments would assume responsibility for such legislation. An ever more complex society,
being relentlessly transformed by the processes of industrialisation and urbanisation, required more sophisticated legislative
solutions to its problems, of a kind that only governments could
realistically attempt. Thus, the 1830s and 1840s saw considerable activity by governments of both parties in areas such as factory and coalmine conditions, public health and education, and
further extensions of state intervention took place during the
mid-Victorian decades. The inevitable consequence was that
governments found it necessary to take over more of Parliament's
time for their measures. If we take the recent figures produced
by Gary Cox, it emerges that divisions in the House of Commons
involving government questions (where the whips, or a whip
and a government minister, acted as tellers) accounted for about
20 per cent of the total in 1832, but then rose rapidly to reach 53
per cent by 1840, and after the 1841 general election it jumped
into the 70–80 per cent range, only dropping to 60–70 per cent
in the years 1850–65.[22] Equally telling of the way that things were
moving after the Great Reform Act was the success of governments in curtailing the rights of back-benchers and securing
priority for ministerial business. In 1835 Mondays and Fridays
became government order days, which meant that the ministerial timetable for measures to be debated on those days of the
week could not be overridden by motions put forward by private members. New Standing Orders (the rules of the House of
Commons) passed in 1842 and 1853 also prevented MPs from
initiating debates on miscellaneous issues when presenting petitions to the House. Furthermore, by another Standing Order
passed in 1852 (and modified in 1866 to close loopholes) governments asserted for themselves a monopoly over the right to
propose new taxation.[23]

Two more important trends, partially pre-dating the Great
Reform Act, were reinforced by changes during the 1830s and
the decades that immediately followed. One of these was the
widespread acceptance by ministers of the 'doctrine of collective
responsibility', which demanded that all members of a government must support all the measures proposed by that
government. Precedents for this 'doctrine' can be traced back
to the 1790s, but the rule does not appear to have been applied

consistently during the early decades of the nineteenth century. An important landmark in the development of this ministerial practice was the censure motion against the policies of the Colonial Secretary, Lord Glenelg, in 1838, when the Foreign Secretary, Palmerston, successfully defended his hapless colleague on the grounds that all ministers were responsible for the government's colonial policy, not just the individual most directly concerned. It was also very rare, by this time, for ministers *ever* to record a dissentient vote on issues of importance to their own government. The reason why collective responsibility was found to be so much more necessary from the 1830s onwards ties in with our previous point, that this was the time when a substantial increase was occurring in the proportion of House of Commons divisions which involved government questions. In other words, the trend towards greater ministerial control of the parliamentary timetable, essential if the heavier load of government legislation was to be carried, was reinforced by a heightened sense of the importance of collective responsibility.[24]

The second major trend which must be considered here involved a group of men whose existence has been referred to several times already – the 'whips'. The early history of whipping is a subject still shrouded in obscurity: what is known is that in the very early years of the nineteenth century a distinction began to evolve between the two Secretaries to the Treasury, with one, eventually to be called the Parliamentary Secretary (or, more commonly, the Patronage Secretary), assuming responsibility for the management of the government's supporters in the House of Commons. It was not until the 1830s, however, that the Parliamentary Secretary to the Treasury, or 'chief whip', concentrated into his own hands all the functions of a modern whip, and it is from this time that it became the established practice for the chief whip to act as a teller in parliamentary divisions involving government questions. (Prior to 1830, it had been common for ministers to do the telling on divisions affecting their own departments.) A link can thus be made between our earlier points, regarding the growth of government legislative activity and the 'doctrine of collective responsibility', and the prominent role of the chief whip. It was also around about 1830 – it is impossible to pinpoint a precise date – that it became customary for the chief whip to have an assistant, and by the 1850s two such 'junior whips' were the norm, usually holding office as Junior Lords of the Treasury.[25]

******

If the scope of the activities of governments was on the increase from the 1830s (but not the effective means of coercing MPs into obedience in the division lobbies), certain parallel developments were taking place on the opposition side. In the case of the Conservative opposition under Sir Robert Peel between 1832 and 1841, which has been studied in some detail, we know that they too had whips, and that an impressive level of disciplined voting was eventually achieved. By 1841, with the Liberal government of Melbourne obviously in a state of terminal decline, the Conservatives were achieving remarkably high levels of attendance and voting cohesion. A series of records kept by the chief whip, Sir Thomas Fremantle, shows for example that on a division on the Irish Registration bill (26 April), only twelve Conservative MPs were absent without a pair, compared with thirty unpaired Liberals, while the following month, in the division on the sugar duties (18 May), just one Conservative was absent unpaired, compared with eighteen Liberals, and whereas one Conservative voted with the government, fourteen Liberals opposed their own leaders. When Peel finally carried a vote of 'no confidence' in ministers, by 312 votes to 311, on 4 June, not a single Conservative was absent without a pair, whereas, crucially, eight Liberals failed to attend the division.[26]

The experience of being thrown into opposition in 1830, after nearly half a century in government, seems to have provided the impetus for the Conservatives to take a number of innovatory steps in the field of extra-parliamentary organisation, which were well in advance of the practices adopted by their ministerial opponents. The foundation of the Carlton Club in 1832, to serve as the party's social and political headquarters, was an important demonstration of the Conservatives' intention to reorganise (the Liberal Reform Club, by contrast, was not founded until 1836, and for years thereafter many MPs did not belong to it.) From 1835, the Conservatives also possessed a permanent party agent, Francis Bonham, who was attached to a permanent election committee headed by Lord Granville Somerset: its function was to collect information from, and provide various forms of assistance to, the growing network of local Conservative associations engaged in electoral work. The Conservatives were ahead of the Liberals not only in terms of central organisation, but also in the willingness of the whips to cultivate links with the press.[27]

After making full allowance for these signs of improved party organisation in the decade after the passing of the Great Reform Act, it is nevertheless contended that the emphasis placed throughout this chapter on the existence of a fluid two-party system provides a better framework in which to understand the ways in which early and mid-Victorian oppositions functioned. We have only to recall the facts that back-bench MPs regularly voted against their leaders, especially on issues of lesser importance, and that the two party front benches often collaborated to block 'extremist' proposals, to see why opposition seldom operated as cohesively, and with the same sense of purpose, as did the Conservatives in the late 1830s and early 1840s. Indeed, it is necessary to stress the point – because it is seldom stated explicitly – that the modern convention that it is legitimate for oppositions to oppose governments for the sake of it, was never accepted in the period we are dealing with. As we shall see in chapter 5, it was not until the 1880s and 1890s that parliamentary politics came to be dominated by the confrontation between government and opposition.

A number of points can be briefly made to help indicate the limits of opposition activity. For instance, it was unusual for oppositions to launch direct attacks upon governments such as motions of 'no confidence': two of the exceptions during our period, the motions of August 1841 and June 1859, occurred immediately after general elections which had shown the government to be in a minority, and were thus a means of delivering the final *coup de grâce* to doomed ministries. Similarly, opposition leaders rarely took the opportunity to challenge governments by moving an amendment to the Address (i.e. during the debate on the Queen's speech) at the beginning of each session. Interestingly enough, major government defeats such as those of January 1855, March 1857 and February 1858 occurred on motions of censure initiated by back-bench radicals, which the opposition party subsequently decided to support. More commonly, oppositions were content to scrutinise and criticise government policies, but refrained from outright resistance in the division lobbies.

They might also focus their attacks upon individual ministers suspected of incompetence or political indiscretion, rather than on the government as a whole: in 1864, two junior ministers, James Stansfeld and Robert Lowe, were accordingly forced to resign, and the following year no less a personage than Lord Westbury, the Lord Chancellor, was driven out of office following allegations of corruption.

In certain institutional respects, too, oppositions functioned in what might seem to us to be a surprisingly lax way. It is true that oppositions had their own whips, but party meetings, at which the leaders met their back-bench followers in order to explain a particular course of action, or to try to raise their morale in difficult times, were infrequent events – rarely more than one or two in any session, and sometimes not at all. (This point applies equally to parties when in government.) On some occasions, leaders were anxious to avoid such gatherings, fearing that they would do more harm than good. It is also seldom appreciated that nothing like a regular 'shadow Cabinet' existed in our period. Occasional meetings of leading oppositionists did take place, but these tended to be *ad hoc* affairs, concerned with settling party tactics on a specific issue, and the attendance varied considerably. In many cases, only a handful of prominent individuals were invited, while at others perhaps as many as twenty or thirty people were involved, going far beyond the boundaries of any supposed body of former or prospective Cabinet members. Furthermore, it was most uncommon for meetings of opposition leaders to include both MPs and peers, a fact that is all the more striking when we remember that the overall leader of an opposition party might well be a peer, as in the case of the 14th Earl of Derby, who led the Conservatives from the Upper House for over twenty years.[28]

Several related factors can help us to understand why the functioning of parliamentary oppositions was so often inhibited. The continued presence of the Crown as an active force in politics is relevant here, more especially because the monarchs of this period were usually known to be supporters of their governments (the glaring exception being William IV's unhappy relationship with Melbourne's administrations between 1834 and 1837). This meant that the opposition, which was normally a Conservative one, found itself in a position where attempts to defeat the government could be construed as disloyalty to the Crown. For a party which drew so much of its sense of identity from its allegiance to the traditional institutions of the country, fear of being considered 'unpatriotic', through a partisan opposition to the ministers of the Crown, was a very real concern. There is no doubt, for example, that Lord Derby in the 1850s was painfully conscious of the fact that the Queen and Prince Albert were hostile to him because of his role in bringing down Peel in 1846.[29] Peel himself, in the 1830s, had been placed in a similarly awkward situation, given his firm adherence to the principles of 'Executive government', and matters became particularly difficult after 1837, when the newly-enthroned teenager, Victoria, developed a strong emotional attachment to her Liberal Prime Minister, Melbourne. It is not at all clear that Peel ever satisfactorily reconciled his general principles of government to the increasingly frequent attacks launched against the Melbourne administration by his own party: one colleague, Sir James Graham, helpfully suggested that the attempt to build up a Conservative majority in the House of Commons should be seen as 'an honest effort to save the Crown against its will'.[30]

The genuine power of the royal prerogative had one further consequence which is pertinent to our consideration of the difficulties facing early and mid-Victorian oppositions. It still rested with the monarch to choose who was to be Prime Minister, and, for this reason, no mechanism existed where a party in opposition could elect or appoint someone as its leader. At times, if there was no outstanding figure such as a former Prime Minister to whom the whole party readily deferred, the consequence could be that a power vacuum was created. It is easily forgotten that in the early 1830s Peel was by no means universally accepted as Conservative leader, and that his position was not secured beyond doubt until William IV asked him to form a government in 1834. An even worse problem of this kind afflicted the Liberals after their fall from power in 1841. The ousted premier, Melbourne, a peer, still had ambitions to return to office, but health problems made this outcome seem highly unlikely: in the mean time, none of the prominent Liberals in the House of Commons enjoyed an unquestioned seniority, with the result that rivals for the leadership like Lord John Russell, Lord Palmerston and Lord Howick sometimes acted independently of one another. This sorry state of confusion in which the Liberals found themselves was described in 1844 by the diarist Charles Greville, who was close to Russell: 'the opposition have no unity of opinion, Howick and John Russell being evidently opposed to each other, and probably all of them entertaining all shades and gradations of opinion'.[31] Once again, it required a commission from the monarch to form a government, in December 1845, to establish that Russell was now the Liberal leader. For a period of over four years, therefore, there had been no official leader of the opposition in the House of Commons.

If the constitutional role of the Crown could sometimes have an inhibiting influence upon the coherence and effectiveness of oppositions, this was often reinforced by the survival of a powerful ideology of 'independence' amongst back-bench MPs. Such 'independence' could take one of two forms. For radicals, it represented a rejection of the whole notion of 'party' *per se*, on the grounds that parties were a manifestation of that corrupt system of aristocratic rule which needed to be swept away. Their ideal was of a House of Commons in which MPs acted as individuals, and where rational debate rather than prejudice and self-interest determined the way MPs voted.[32] In practice, the radicals' determination to assert their independence of party ties meant that they had little compunction about embarrassing the Liberal leadership at any time, but particularly when the party was in opposition. Thus, in the one period between the first and second Reform Acts when the Liberals were in opposition because they were in a minority in the House of Commons, from 1841 to 1846, maverick radicals like Roebuck and Hume were repeatedly to be found initiating debates and forcing divisions on such issues as the causes of the Afghan war, the government of India and the abolition of the post of Lord Lieutenant of Ireland, and just as invariably they were opposed by Russell and other Liberal leaders, as well as by the Conservative government.

However, the ideology and rhetoric of 'independence' operated equally strongly, but in a very different way, on the Conservative side of politics. The thinking of many Conservatives was still deeply influenced by the eighteenth-century doctrine of civic humanism, which envisaged a virtuous polity controlled by men of substance who were above the temptation of corruption. In the civic humanist ideal, party connections could only be legitimate provided they were based upon the common pursuit of shared principles. What was emphatically not permissible was an opportunistic combination of groups of politicians with conflicting principles.[33] It is easy to see how this ideology of 'independence' intertwined with reverence for the Crown to produce a Conservative mind-set that was disposed to favour government conducted in the 'national interest', and was suspicious of opposition conduct which appeared to be purely factious. This made the notion of blatant opposition for opposition's sake unpalatable for many Conservatives, and it was therefore imperative for the party leaders that they should not give the appearance of having a factious intent, and that they should endeavour to employ the language of 'disinterestedness'. In times of national crisis, such as the Crimean War of 1854–56, we consequently find the Conservative whips urging very strongly the need for the opposition to show restraint, as many MPs were not prepared to support any action that might endanger the government. As Edward Taylor, a junior whip, put it in the autumn of 1855, 'So long as war lasts, & is made a national question, politics and party will be secondary considerations, & the boundary lines that divide the sections have become already less perceptible'.[34] Mid-Victorian Conservative fears that their conduct in opposition might be unprincipled, and therefore unvirtuous by the standards of civic humanism, were naturally heightened by the propensity of their deeply distrusted House of Commons leader, Benjamin Disraeli, to seek out opportunistic alliances with alien political groups such as the radicals and the Irish Roman Catholics. As late as May 1862 we find a junior Liberal whip noting with satisfaction that attempts by Disraeli to bid for the support of the radicals, by making speeches in favour of retrenchment in government expenditure, and at the same time to appeal to Irish MPs by making comments sympathetic to the Pope, had all backfired:

> D'Israeli's cause ... has evidently damaged him with his own party, both Tories & Protestants. This was somewhat shown by the faintness of the cheers which greeted him in these speeches, & still more by the division upon the vote for the Harbour at Alderney, which he opposed altho' it was only the continuation of the grant which his own government had proposed and supported when in office. Nearly as many Conservatives (& amongst them

General Peel [former Secretary for War]) voted with Government as with D'Israeli, & on a second division being taken on the 'Report' of the same vote, when Government increased their majority from 8 to 56, 54 Tories followed D'Israeli, & 45 supported Government.[35]

The perils of Disraeli's tactic of 'dallying' with the radicals were made clear the following month, when an opposition motion calling for retrenchment collapsed ignominiously after Palmerston made it clear that he regarded the vote as one of confidence in his government.[36]

Notions of 'Executive government' and of the 'independence' of MPs thus operated powerfully against the effective use of systematic or unprincipled opposition for much of the time, but the realities described by the co-existing idea of 'Parliamentary government' also played a part in restricting the action of oppositions. There was no escaping the fact that, even if the monarch still had some influence over the appointment of an individual as Prime Minister, changes of government in themselves were nearly always brought about by shifts in the balance of party support in the House of Commons. Only in 1841 would it be accurate to say that a general election, by producing a decisive shift in support from the government to the opposition, led to a change of government, though even on this occasion Melbourne followed constitutional convention by waiting for his government to be defeated in the new House of Commons before he actually resigned.[37] The implication of this point is that for an opposition leader seeking to displace a government, in the early and mid-Victorian period, it was futile simply to wait for the next general election, and a 'swing of the pendulum' (a phrase not widely used until the 1880s), to bring about the desired result. If a government was to be removed from office, therefore, the most likely way of achieving this was by effecting a disintegration of that government's following in the House of Commons. But, as we shall see, opposition leaders often calculated that the best chance of breaking up the governing party lay not in all-out attacks upon it, but by the very opposite tactic – refraining from attacks, and perhaps even supporting the government.

Sir Robert Peel's career as leader of the opposition, up to 1841, is entirely misunderstood if it is conceived solely in terms of the building-up of a party through improved extra-parliamentary organisation and electoral gains. On the contrary, in the aftermath of the disastrous election defeat of 1832, following the passage of the Great Reform Act, Peel understood clearly that the future recovery of the Conservative Party depended on its ability to win over support from among the diverse coalition of government supporters. In 1834 he described the situation as he saw it, to one of his colleagues, in the following way: 'How can the Conservative party, if again called to the Government, hope to maintain itself, except by conciliating the goodwill, at least by mitigating the hostility, of many of the more moderate and respectable supporters of the present Government?' Unprincipled alliances with incompatible groups like the radicals, simply for the purpose of gaining a short-term victory over the government, were therefore to be avoided. What Peel hoped to see happen was a collapse of the government 'through its own differences and misunderstandings', which would then enable the Conservatives to take office with a much better chance of securing support from alarmed moderate Liberals.[38] This thinking provides the essential context for understanding Peel's well-known strategy of 'governing in opposition', that is to say, lending his support to ministers so that they were strong enough to resist radical pressure for measures such as the introduction of secret ballot, further extensions of the franchise, and the repeal of the Corn Laws.[39] By pursuing this course, Peel was able to present himself as a patriot and a statesman, but at the same time it was possible to achieve his ulterior objects of aggravating the friction between the government and its radical back-benchers, and of drawing off the government's more moderate supporters. Peel's strategy never succeeded entirely, for he had to wait until after the 1841 general election before he could take office with a clear parliamentary majority, but it is highly significant that in the years between 1832 and 1841 nearly sixty MPs had crossed over the floor of the House of Commons to join the Conservatives.[40]

The period of Liberal opposition between 1841 and 1846 has hardly been studied at all by historians, but there is enough evidence to suggest that the Conservative opposition strategy just described was also adopted by the Liberals. Initial attacks on Peel's government, notably over the introduction of the income tax in 1842, served only to bring out the natural instinct for Conservative back-benchers to rally round their leader in the face of hostile opposition action. Consequently, by June 1843, we find one front-bench Liberal, Sir John Cam Hobhouse, noting in his diary that 'everyone says the party ought to be quiet & allow the Ministerialists to quarrel among themselves.'[41] Since the Liberals were already expending a great deal of energy in quarrelling among *themselves*, this was probably a sensible strategy. At any rate, the Conservatives eventually obliged, for in 1845 they were split in half over the question of the Maynooth grant, which Peel was only able to carry with Liberal assistance. And of course, in the following year, more than two-thirds of Conservative MPs voted against the repeal of the Corn Laws, which also required opposition support in order to pass, but on this occasion the Liberals, having helped to create a chasm in the Conservative ranks, drove home their advantage by joining with a rump of rebel Conservatives to defeat the government on its Irish Coercion bill, thus forcing Peel's resignation. The events of 1846 provide a classic illustration of the way an opposition party could gain office, not by winning a general election, but by seizing an opportunity to wreck the government's parliamentary following.

It was during the twenty years of almost permanent Conservative opposition under Lord Derby's leadership,[42] following the Corn Law crisis of 1846, that the deliberate strategy of avoiding factious attacks on the government, and thereby endeavouring to exacerbate the inevitable divisions of opinion within the governing majority, was stated in its most explicit form. With the benefit of hindsight, it is tempting to think of the mid-Victorian era as one of natural Liberal domination of politics, but this was never seen to be the case by the Conservatives at the time, because the fissiparous nature of the Liberals' back-bench following appeared to offer plenty of scope for an eventual realignment of forces which might bring Derby and his colleagues securely into power. In the early 1850s, for example, it was still possible to entertain hopes that leading Peelites such as Gladstone and Sidney Herbert could be brought back into the Conservative fold, and that perhaps prominent Liberals, above all Lord Palmerston, could be enticed across the floor of the House of Commons. Accordingly, when a Liberal/Peelite coalition government was formed with Lord Aberdeen as Premier, in December 1852, Derby confided to his son that the Conservatives' approach towards the new government should be: 'Wait – don't attack Ministers – that will only bind them together – if left alone they must fall to pieces by their own disunion'.[43] Indeed, the Aberdeen coalition duly collapsed, under the pressures of the Crimean War, early in 1855, and at this point Derby calculated on being able to recruit Palmerston and some Peelites into a Conservative ministry.[44] Unfortunately for him, it turned out that Palmerston was able to put together an alternative Liberal government, and over the next few years managed to consolidate the union between Liberals and Peelites. Even so, the potential for opening up divisions within the Liberal ranks, between ministers and their more radical supporters, remained considerable, and given Palmerston's advanced age (born in 1784, he was fifteen years older than Derby), the Conservative leader was always inclined to persist with his strategy of patience and moderation. Shortly after the 1857 general election, Derby wrote to his lieutenant in the House of Commons, Disraeli, urging that the opposition's policy should be to encourage Palmerston to rely as much as possible on Conservative rather than radical support:

> to foment divisions and jealousies between the discordant elements of the Government majority must be our first object; while we should carefully avoid multiplying occasions for their voting in concert, in opposition to measures brought forward by us ... among Palmerstonians ... there are as strong Conservatives at heart as any in our ranks; and looking to Palmerston's increased age and infirmities, the oftener these can be brought into the same lobby in opposition to Radical moves, the better for us.[45]

Derby was seeking to continue this long-term strategy when, in 1860 and again in 1861, he informed Palmerston, through an intermediary, that the Conservatives would not vote against his government if it was threatened by the radicals on specified issues like finance or parliamentary reform (see Doc. 22). The object, of course, was to encourage Palmerston to resist radical demands in the knowledge that he could rely on Conservative support to save him, but had he accepted Derby's offer he would have run a grave risk of destroying the fragile unity of his own parliamentary following. In the event, Palmerston proved adroit enough to avoid falling between the two stools of radical and Conservative support, and he remained in office until his death in October

1865. Derby's strategy can, in this obvious sense, be judged a failure, but it was arguably the only rational response that he could have made given the political environment in which he had to operate. It is surely significant that even Disraeli, renowned for his love of unprincipled parliamentary manoeuvring, recognised the validity of Derby's approach, and often followed it himself, especially in the last years of the Palmerston regime: surprising as it may seem, Disraeli only voted in eight out of 188 Commons divisions in 1863, seventeen out of 156 in 1864, and nine out of 104 in 1865.[46]

Paradoxically, then, the restraints imposed upon overtly partisan behaviour by opposition parties, arising from the looseness of party ties and from the prevailing ideologies of the time, did not prevent opposition from systematically pursuing a strategy designed to bring about the downfall of the governing party. Co-operation between the government and opposition front benches undoubtedly reflected the desire for political consensus within the traditional ruling class, but it could also be used to achieve partisan objectives. The importance of establishing this point justifies the considerable space that has been devoted to studying the workings of parliamentary opposition.

******

Though the main focus in this chapter has been on government and opposition, and the ways in which the rival Liberal and Conservative parties operated given the limited nature of the two-party system, it will have become apparent that there were also a number of minor 'parties', or at any rate groupings of MPs, functioning at various times within the parliamentary arena. A brief survey of these minor 'parties' seems worthwhile as a means of concluding our study of the early and mid-Victorian period, for their respective fates serve to confirm the overall impression of a two-party system which was certainly fluid, but which at the same time had an undeniably powerful magnetic pull.

At regular intervals during the period between the first and second Reform Acts, there was talk of the radicals on the left of the Liberal political spectrum breaking away and forming a separate party. Such talk rarely, however, crystallised into positive action. In the early months of 1835, definite plans were being hatched for an independent party of some seventy or eighty radicals, but the scheme soon broke down amidst disagreements as to who should be invited to join it (some strongly objected to the proposed inclusion of the Irish Nationalist leader, Daniel O'Connell), and in any case the project had been weakened by the unwillingness of some prominent figures to participate in a body that was to act entirely separately from the main Liberal leadership. Some years later, in the spring of 1848, a group of fifty or so radicals did declare themselves to be an independent party, and they issued their 'little Charter', a watered-down version of the Chartists' demands, but there is no sign of this radical party continuing to act together beyond the 1848 session of Parliament. Another short-lived phenomenon was the group of so-called 'independent Liberals', allegedly 120 in number and with their own whip, which existed for the duration of the minority Conservative administration of 1858–59, and aimed to prevent the restoration of Palmerston as Liberal Prime Minister. It totally failed in its object.[47] Significantly, two of these radical movements arose in brief periods – 1835 and 1858–59 – when the Liberal Party was thrown into opposition, and neither was able to resist the pressures of party loyalty generated once the prospect of a return to office appeared. Furthermore, the anti-party ideology shared by many radicals, which was discussed earlier, militated against organised action for any length of time: they might consistently denounce the aristocratic corruption inherent in the existing party system, but the formation of a 'radical party' was, by their own standards, a contradiction in terms. The radicals were, by their very nature, far too individualistic, quarrelsome and competitive, and had far too many rival projects and conflicting priorities, to work together as an effective team, a fact that was recognised even by a sympathetic journalist like E. M. Whitty: 'the Radicals are all clever or crotchety – and they are, therefore, an army of captains . . . which, when the battle begins, is certain to radiate into adventurous isolations . . . Each Knight has his own banner, and cries his own cry . . . Party completeness is sacrificed to personal glory'.[48] From the point of view of the Liberal leadership, of course, this state of affairs was all to the good. Parliamentary radicalism generally functioned as a semi-detached, semi-hostile, body of opinion on the benches 'below the gangway', frequently sniping at the Liberal leadership, but all the same providing a drudging support in many moments of need, when the alternative would have been a Conservative government. Their support for Liberal administrations could never be taken for granted, however, and so a sense of precarious existence regularly afflicted these administrations. Prior to the 1861 session of Parliament, for instance, fifty-one MPs signed a circular calling for retrenchment in military expenditure, and the Liberal chief whip reckoned that perhaps sixteen of them 'may have signed from *mischief*', to which could be added the names of the instigators of the circular, Cobden and Bright. In the right circumstances, this body of radicals would have been numerous enough to deprive Palmerston's government of its majority in the division lobby. As a junior Liberal whip noted, shortly after the session began, 'A portion of the Radicals ... would join any day in an attempt to overthrow us, & the opportunity may arise at any moment'.[49]

Liberal leaderships faced similar problems with MPs from Ireland who, although at least nominally Liberal in their politics, were mainly Roman Catholic in religion and sympathetic to nationalist aspirations. In the early 1830s a group of around forty Irish members, supporters of Daniel O'Connell and his campaign for the repeal of the Act of Union between Britain and Ireland (hence their name 'repealers'), operated in a semi-independent relationship with Earl Grey's government. Later in the decade, however, after the so-called 'Lichfield House compact' of 1835, O'Connell moved into a position of regular support for the Liberals, and the repealers dwindled in number as many succumbed to the lure of government patronage. Even so, Lord John Russell in the 1840s continued to experience difficulties with the Irish Liberals, particularly when his government resorted to the use of coercion in Ireland in 1848, and a formal breach occurred in 1850 when Russell adopted an anti-papal stance on the question of the reintroduction of a Roman Catholic hierarchy into England. During the 1850s, in consequence, an independent Irish party existed, known as the 'Irish Brigade', which for a time appeared formidable through its links with the agrarian movement for tenant right in Ireland. After the 1852 general election the Brigade was perhaps forty-eight strong in the House of Commons, but its organisation and leadership were weak (O'Connell had died in 1847), and by 1857 its number had dwindled to about fourteen. When the Liberals, Peelites and radicals met at Willis's rooms in June 1859, and agreed to work together, the Irish Brigade played no part because they were offended by Liberal support for the Risorgimento in Italy, which threatened the temporal power of the Pope. Up to the mid-1860s, therefore, the Irish Brigade remained a loosely organised group, alienated from the Palmerston regime, and ready enough to prove their nuisance value in the division lobbies. But, at the same time, the widespread feeling amongst British politicians of all shades, including the radicals, that the Irish were a drunken, superstitious, alien and incomprehensible breed, tended to restrict the scope for effective co-operation.[50]

On the Conservative side of the House of Commons there was nothing that could properly be described as an organised 'wing' of the party after the mid-1830s, once the so-called 'Ultras', those who had been alienated from the leadership by the surrender on Catholic Emancipation in 1829, were reintegrated into the main body.[51] Of far greater potential interest, during this decade, was the role of a group of centrist politicians known as the 'Derby Dilly'. This group emerged in 1834 when four members of Lord Grey's Cabinet, Sir James Graham, the Duke of Richmond, Lord Ripon and Lord Stanley, resigned because of differences with their colleagues on the question of the Irish Church. The key figure in the Dilly was Stanley (he was the heir of the Earl of Derby – hence the nickname 'Derby Dilly' – and we have already encountered him as the leader of the Conservatives after 1846), the outstanding parliamentary orator of his generation, and a man who clearly aspired to the premiership. Indeed, when William IV dismissed Melbourne's government, in November 1834, he would have been perfectly entitled to ask Stanley, rather than Peel, to form the alternative government. In the event, Stanley's dream of heading a centrist coalition government of moderate Liberals and moderate Conservatives was spoiled by the king's choice of Peel, which enabled the latter to consolidate his position as leader of the Conservative Party. Stanley and his friends declined Peel's offer of posts in his government, but they were gradually drawn towards the Conservative Party during the next two to three years. The Derby Dilly was never an organised 'third party' – at one point, early in 1835, Stanley made a list of thirty-seven Liberal MPs who he believed would follow him, but some of these never left the Liberal fold – and Stanley's hopes for the premiership depended on a favourable act of the royal prerogative, which never happened. Instead, the Dilly merely contributed to a wider process of moderate Liberal drifting towards Peel during the 1830s.[52]

A more famous group of centrist politicians were, of course, the 'Peelites', those Conservatives who supported the repeal of the Corn Laws in 1846 and therefore became estranged from the majority of 'Protectionists' in their party. Given that there were originally some 120 Conservative MPs who had supported Peel, the material was apparently available for him to organise a formidable 'third party', which would undoubtedly have held the balance of power in the House of Commons. However, Peel showed no desire to build up another party, in spite of urgings from some of his more zealous followers, and in the last four years of his life he was generally content to give Lord John Russell's Liberal ministry an independent support, in order to ensure that the government of the country did not fall into the hands of the Protectionists. To talk of a 'Peelite party' in the late 1840s, therefore, is misleading: rather, we should envisage a body of like-minded MPs, perhaps thirty or at most forty of whom formed a hard core and occasionally managed to concert their actions, while the rest were basically unaligned and waited to see how Peel and the Protectionist leader, Derby, behaved. In fact, by 1852, as the prospect of a Derbyite attempt to restore protectionism receded, about one-third of the Free Trade Conservatives had rejoined the ranks of Derby's party, and further drifting occurred subsequently.[53] A few 'Peelites' threw in their lot with the Liberals in the mean time, and, combined with the effects of death and retirement, the result was that by 1857 only a tiny group of Peelites survived – essentially a handful of chiefs without many Indians. The final absorption of the Peelites took place in 1859, when Gladstone and Herbert (plus a peer, the Duke of Newcastle), agreed to serve in Palmerston's administration.

The fate of the various splinter groups, and semi-independent sections, described here provides valuable support for the central argument of this chapter, that a two-party system, however loosely it may have functioned at times, was a reality for the whole of the period between the first and second Reform Acts.

Radicals, Irish Brigades, Dillies and Peelites were all in evidence, but there was no general political fragmentation, even after 1846, and the essential point remains that none of the groups mentioned were able to act for very long independently of the two main parties. Only the Peelites *might* have become a real 'third party', if Peel had been inclined to organise and lead them (see Doc. 18). For the rest, the choice was always going to be between active participation within one of the main parties, or sulky ineffectuality on the sidelines of politics.

Notes

1 In February 1851, February 1852, December 1852, January 1855, February 1858 and June 1859. On the first of these occasions, Russell's government was reinstated. In addition, Palmerston's government was defeated on a censure motion, in March 1857, but a dissolution of Parliament followed.

2 For example, Norman Gash, *Aristocracy and People, 1815–1865* (London, 1979), chs 6 and 9.

3 David Close, 'The Formation of a Two-Party Alignment in the House of Commons between 1832 and 1841', *English Historical Review*, LXXXIV (1969), pp. 257–77; D. E. D. Beales, 'Parliamentary Parties and the "Independent" Member, 1810–1860', in Robert Robson (ed.), *Ideas and Institutions of Victorian Britain* (London, 1967), pp. 1–19.

4 Edward Baines Jnr, *The Life of Edward Baines* (London, 1851), p. 192.

5 Ian Newbould, *Whiggery and Reform, 1830–1841* (London, 1990), pp. 16–23. Newbould used 'touchstone' divisions, of the kind focused on by Close, to establish MPs' Liberal affiliation.

6 D. R. Fisher, 'Peel and the Conservative Party: The Sugar Crisis of 1844 Reconsidered', *Historical Journal*, XVIII (1975), pp. 279–302, an article of wider significance than its title suggests.

7 In his pioneering statistical analysis of MPs voting behaviour in the Parliament of 1841–47, W. O. Aydelotte showed that relatively few issues produced a straightforward two-party voting pattern, but he also made the crucial point that simply because parties were divided on many issues, this ought not to be interpreted as proof of a state of near-anarchy in the House of Commons. On the contrary, he established that the division of opinion on any given issue frequently affected one party much more than the other. To give just two examples from many, when the House voted in May 1842 on the question of whether to debate the Chartist petition, the Liberals were seriously split, but the Conservatives were unanimously hostile; but on the removal of Jewish disabilities, in July 1845, the Liberals were unanimously in favour and the

Conservatives split. Each party, in other words, was internally divided on a number of issues, but this was not inconsistent with the existence of a two-party alignment based on ideological differences, and MPs voting behaviour was related to their party allegiances. Paradoxically, the evidence for a limited two-party pattern helped to confirm that a two-party voting system was functioning; 'Parties and Issues in Early Victorian England', *Journal of British Studies*, V (1966), pp. 95–114.

8 Hugh Berrington, 'Partisanship and Dissidence in the Nineteenth Century House of Commons', *Parliamentary Affairs*, XXI (1968), p. 344. The total percentages sometimes exceed 100 because of the rounding of individual figures. 1836 was the first year in which official division lists were produced.

9 Ian Newbould, 'Sir Robert Peel and the Conservative party, 1832–1841: A Study in Failure?', *English Historical Review*, XCVIII (1983), pp. 529–57.

10 Berrington, 'Partisanship and Dissidence', p. 361.

11 T. A. Jenkins, *The Liberal Ascendancy, 1830–1886* (London, 1994), ch. 2.

12 Brand to Gladstone, 8 May 1860 and 15 July 1863, BL Add MSS 44193, fos 24, 69–71.

13 Robert Stewart, *The Foundation of the Conservative Party, 1830–1867* (London, 1978), pp. 312–14; P. M. Gurowich, 'The Continuation of War by Other Means: Party and Politics, 1855–1865', *Historical Journal*, XXVII (1984), p. 620 and n. 115; T. A. Jenkins (ed.), *The Parliamentary Diaries of Sir John Trelawny, 1858–1865*, (Royal Historical Society, Camden Fourth Series, vol. 40, 1990), 24 July 1860, 11 March 1861, 1 August 1862, 18 April 1864, 2 March 1865, 2 May 1865.

14 D. E. D. Beales, *England and Italy, 1859–60* (London, 1961), p. 82; David F. Krein, *The Last Palmerston Government* (Iowa, 1978), pp. 168–9.

15 Taylor to Disraeli, 30 August [1861], and enclosed list, Hughenden MSS (Bodleian Library, Oxford), B/XX/T/18 and 143. Cf. the analysis of voting patterns by Valerie Cromwell, 'Mapping the political world of 1861: A multidimensional analysis of House of Commons divisions lists', *Legislative Studies Quarterly*, VII (1982), pp. 281–97.

16 John Hogan, 'Party Management in the House of Lords, 1846–1865', *Parliamentary History*, X (1991), pp. 124–50.

17 Philip Ziegler, *Melbourne* (London, 1976), pp. 256–317.

18 Speech in the House of Commons, 17 September 1841, Norman Gash (ed.), *The Age of Peel* (London, 1968), pp. 87–8.

19 C. H. Stuart, 'The Prince Consort and Ministerial Politics, 1856–9', in H. R. Trevor-Roper (ed.), *Essays Presented to Sir Keith Feiling* (London, 1964), pp. 247–69.

20 This paragraph is indebted to the stimulating article by Angus Hawkins, ' "Parliamentary Government" and Victorian Political Parties, c.1830–c.1880', *English Historical Review*, CIV (1989), pp. 638–69.

21 Walter Bagehot, *The English Constitution*, ed. R. H. S. Crossman (London, 1963), pp. 150–1.

22 Gary Cox, 'The Development of Collective Responsibility in the United Kingdom', *Parliamentary History*, XIII (1994), pp. 32–47. Cox's method of analysis differs slightly from that in his earlier article, 'The Origin of Whip Votes in the House of Commons', *Parliamentary History*, XI (1992), pp. 278–85.

23 Peter Fraser, 'The Growth of Ministerial Control in the Nineteenth Century House of Commons', *English Historical Review*, LXXV (1960), pp. 444–63.

24 Cox, 'Development of Collective Responsibility', pp. 42–7.

25 J. C. Sainty, 'The Evolution of the Parliamentary and Financial Secretaryships of the Treasury', *English Historical Review*, XCI (1976), pp. 566–84; Cox, 'Development of Collective Responsibility', pp. 39–41. For the connection between Junior Lords of the Treasury and the whips, by the 1850s, see the unpublished dissertation by P. M. Gurowich, 'Party and Independence in the early and mid-Victorian House of Commons' University of Cambridge (1986), pp. 89–96.

26 Fremantle MSS (Bucks RO), D/FR/110/9. For earlier examples, see Stewart, *Foundation of Conservative Party*, Appendix 5.

27 Norman Gash, 'The Organisation of the Conservative Party, 1832–1846. Part I: The Parliamentary Organisation. Part II: The Electoral Organisation', *Parliamentary History*, I (1982), pp. 137–59, II (1983), pp. 131–52; Ian Newbould, 'Whiggery and the Growth of Party 1830–1841: Organisation and the Challenge of Reform', *Parliamentary History*, IV (1985), pp. 137–56.

28 Cf. D. R. Turner, *The Shadow Cabinet in British Politics* (London, 1969), pp. 1–34; R. M. Punnett, *Front-Bench Opposition* (London, 1973), pp. 39–45.

29 J. R. Vincent (ed.), *Disraeli, Derby and the Conservative Party: The Political Journals of Lord Stanley, 1849–69* (Brighton, 1978), pp. 39, 47, 53.

30 Graham to Peel, 26 December 1839, in C. S. Parker (ed.), *Sir Robert Peel: From his Private Papers*, 3 vols (London, 1891–99), ii, 427–9.

31 Henry Reeve (ed.), *The Greville Memoirs*, 8 vols (London, 1888), 8 February 1844.

32 R. McGowen and W. Arnstein, 'The Mid-Victorians and the Two-Party System', *Albion*, XI (1979), pp. 242–58.

33 See the invaluable analysis in P. M. Gurowich's dissertation, 'Party and Independence in the early and mid-Victorian House of Commons' (Cambridge, 1986), pp. 99–190.

34 Taylor to Jolliffe, 14 October [1855], Hylton MSS (Somerset RO), DD/HY/24/21/1; cf. G. A. Hamilton to Jolliffe, 28 November [1854], *ibid.*, DD/HY/18/11/10.

35   Diary of Edward Knatchbull Hugessen, 27 May 1862, Brabourne MSS (Kent RO), U951/F27/1.

36   *Ibid.*, 20 June 1862.

37   It is true that in 1835, 1852 and 1859 changes of government took place shortly after general elections, but each of these cases involved a Conservative government that had been in a minority *before* the election.

38   Peel to Goulburn, 25 May 1834, in Parker, *Sir Robert Peel*, ii, 243–4. For similar views, see Stanley to Peel, 19 February 1838, and Wellington to Peel, 22 February 1838, *ibid.*, ii, 361–4.

39   Newbould, 'Sir Robert Peel and the Conservative Party', notes that this strategy also had the advantage of curbing the 'ultras' within the Conservative ranks.

40   Stewart, *Foundation of Conservative Party*, Appendices 2 and 4.

41   *Greville Memoirs*, 23 March 1842; diary of J. C. Hobhouse, 26 June 1843, BL Add MSS 43745.

42   He was raised to the peerage as Baron Stanley in 1844, and did not succeed to the Earldom of Derby until 1851, but I shall refer to him throughout as Derby.

43   *Stanley Journals*, p. 94.

44   *Ibid.*, 'Memorandum on the Change of Ministry, January-February 1855'.

45   Derby to Disraeli, 24 April 1857, in W. F. Monypenny and G. E. Buckle, *The Life of Benjamin Disraeli*, 2 vol. edn. (London, 1929), i, 1480–1.

46   Gurowich, 'Party and Politics, 1855–1865', pp. 621–7; also Angus Hawkins, 'Lord Derby and Victorian Conservatism: A Reappraisal', *Parliamentary History*, VI (1987), pp. 280–301. Together these provide a corrective to the account in Stewart, *Foundation of Conservative Party*, pp. 310–18.

47   For these various radical groups, see Jenkins, *Liberal Ascendancy*, pp. 21, 63–7, 88.

48   E. M. Whitty, *St Stephen's in the Fifties*, ed. Justin McCarthy (London, 1906), pp. 18–27.

49   Circular and list, dated 15 January 1861, and Brand to Palmerston, 20 January 1861, Brand MSS (HLRO), vol. I; diary of Edward Knatchbull Hugessen, 26 February 1861, Brabourne MSS, U951/F27/1.

50   A. D. Macintyre, *The Liberator: Daniel O'Connell and the Irish Party, 1830–1847* (London, 1965); J. H. Whyte, *The Independent Irish Party, 1850–9* (Oxford, 1958).

51   Stewart, *Foundation of Conservative Party*, pp. 98–104.

52   *Ibid.*, pp. 110–17 and Appendix 3.

53   Gurowich, 'Party and Politics, 1855–1865', p. 606 and n. 24; J. B. Conacher, *The Peelites and the Party System, 1846–52* (Newton Abbot, 1972); W. D. Jones and A. B. Erickson, *The Peelites, 1846–57* (Ohio, 1972).

3

Whips and back-benchers

To a radically-inclined observer of the parliamentary scene in the 1850s, William White, it appeared that the most powerful man in the House of Commons was not the Prime Minister, or the leader of the opposition, but the government's chief 'whipper-in', William Goodenough Hayter. White's reasoning was very simple: 'Palmerston and Disraeli make long speeches. Mr. Hayter flourishes figuratively a long and formidable whip – and the whip is very much more effective than the most eloquent harangues. A good speech may possibly change the mind of some two or three members during a debate, but Mr. Hayter, by his more effective logic, brings up scores of sluggish members to the division'.[1] It was the case, after all, that typically no more than one-half of the MPs voting in any particular division had actually listened to the relevant debate, the rest coming in from the tea rooms and committee rooms, or from their London clubs or some society entertainment in order to cast their votes, and being content to follow the instructions of the party whips. Exactly how the whips' 'mysterious arts and powerful incantations' were applied remained a closely-kept secret, but 'that they are of wondrous power is certain and not to be disputed. Many a fond dream of independence have they dissipated, and many an indignant patriotic feeling have they damped down'.[2]

William White's accounts of the whips' activities have helped to popularise the shadowy, sinister reputation attaching to these practitioners of the political equivalent of the 'black arts'. During the twentieth century, their notoriety has been greatly enhanced by frequent complaints about the subjugation of back-bench MPs who have allegedly become nothing more than galley slaves, terrified of arousing the wrath of their masters. While this is un-doubtedly an exaggeration even of the contemporary reality, it is nevertheless true that MPs today are far more dependent on their parties than was the case with their Victorian predecessors. In a very literal sense, MPs in the nineteenth century did not owe their seats to the goodwill of the party managers. They were expected to foot the bill for their own electoral contests (only very limited central resources were ever available to provide subsidies for deserving candidates), which, prior to the Corrupt Practices Act of 1883, could easily amount to many thousands of pounds. Possession of independent financial means was there-fore virtually a prerequisite for a man's election to the House of Commons, and this was one of the main reasons why, until the 1880s, the composition of the House was dominated by gentlemen from the aristocratic and landed class (see chapter 4 for further details). Furthermore, the secure social and financial background of most MPs meant that they were not necessarily ambitious for political office, so that Victorian whips did not have readily available to them the sanction that promotion might be withheld from an MP who disobeyed the party line – a potent weapon in the armoury of a modern-day whip. For these reasons, it was possible for an MP to make genuine claims for his own 'independence', even though, as we saw in chapter 2, he was almost certain to be identified with one or other of the political parties. Clearly, the relationship between Victorian MPs and their parties was of a very different nature from that to which we are accustomed today, and a study of how the whips operated will indeed suggest that even William White's description of their occult practices is misleading.

It should be noted that the following discussion of the whips' role in parliamentary management is only dealing with one part of their job, for they also had overall charge of election man-agement, which made their office an exceptionally burdensome one. So far as their parliamentary responsibilities are concerned, it was the whips' task to ensure a sufficient attendance by MPs to support the actions of the party leaders, whether it be minis-ters seeking to push through their legislation, or the opposition endeavouring to launch an attack on the government. To this end,

circulars were sent out by the whips, on behalf of the party leaders, before the start of each parliamentary session, notifying MPs
of the date when Parliament was due to meet and requesting
their presence in London at that time. During the session numerous notes, which came to be known as 'whips', would be issued,
urging members to attend the House in order to vote on specific
issues. On the Conservative side, in the late 1830s, there were a
number of complaints from MPs about the unreliability of the
information contained in the whips' notes, with claims that they
often gave a misleading impression of the necessity for attendance,[3] but this does not appear to have been a serious problem
in subsequent years. Having endeavoured to ensure that members were in London at the required time, a good deal of effort
was still involved in securing a good turn-out *in* the House of
Commons, and it was also the whips' function to act as tellers
(i.e. counters) when divisions took place.

The papers of Sir William Jolliffe, Conservative chief whip
from 1853 until 1860, are the richest source of evidence on the
effort involved in whipping-up members, containing as they do
numerous letters from his assistants, Colonel Edward Taylor
and George Alexander Hamilton. Securing a good attendance at
the beginning of each parliamentary session seems to have provided the Conservative whips with one of their biggest headaches.
Some MPs preferred to spend the winter months in Continental
resorts, like Nice, and made it clear that their attendance at Westminster could not be counted on until after the Easter re-
cess.[4] MPs from Ireland were understandably reluctant to make
the journey to London any earlier than was strictly necessary,
as Taylor (himself an Irishman) advised Jolliffe on one occasion:
'No end of our men are wanting to know whether they *must*
be up in town for the 3rd and saying that they will not if they
can help it. Some of these will not tolerate *squeezing* – & I think it
will be prudent not to write to them unless *really* wanted'.[5] Then
there was the inevitable problem, for the party of the landed
interest, of avoiding undue inconvenience to 'the hunting men and
country-loving members'.[6] Interestingly, a collective effort was
sometimes resorted to in order to shame and cajole members
into attending on the required date, as Taylor reported to his
chief early in 1854: 'Having consulted with George Hamilton I
have made out a list of about forty men with whom I am pretty

intimate & who for various causes can influence others, to whom I propose to write a private letter, asking them to assist as far as lies in their power to induce those who call themselves our friends to attend'.[7]

Patience and persistence continued to be essential virtues for a whip during the course of a parliamentary session, and we find various devices being applied, for example, when the Conservatives resolved to oppose the bill to reform Oxford University in 1854. Taylor's advice was that 'I would not trust to printed *whips* to get our men up – but write private letters to those who require most pressure', while at the same time peer-group pressure should be brought to bear, by 'making the more zealous of our people work as agents to screw up the idle'.[8] The correspondence of a later Conservative chief whip, Aretas Akers Douglas, indicates that even in the altered circumstances of the 1880s, when MPs were accountable to much wider electorates, there was remarkably little the whips could do to combat the capriciousness of certain members. During the tumultuous parliamentary session of 1887, in which Lord Salisbury's government was seeking to carry an Irish coercion bill and an Irish Land bill in the face of often furious opposition, reliable attendance by Conservative MPs was of paramount importance, but Akers Douglas learned of a member who would not attend a debate on the coercion bill because it seemed likely to last a whole week, another who was in camp with the volunteer army and unavailable unless absolutely required, another who was prepared to come up to London to vote on specified issues but nothing else, and, by way of compensation, a member who announced that he would be able to attend the House of Commons after all, since his plan to hire a grouse moor had fallen through.[9]

The truth of the matter was that there was very little the whips could do to discipline unco-operative or disobedient MPs, because most of them were not dependent on their party for the possession of their seats. In December 1854, for instance, Parliament was summoned early to consider special legislation required by the Aberdeen coalition government for the conduct of the Crimean War, including a Foreign Enlistment bill, allowing the recruitment of foreign mercenaries who would be trained in Britain. This measure was denounced by the opposition leaders as an unconstitutional proceeding, but the bill survived the divisions on its second and third readings thanks to the absence of substantial numbers of Conservative members. What was particularly provoking, from the whips' point of view, was that not only were forty-seven Conservatives absent without good cause from the second reading division, but thirty-three who had voted did not bother to stay in London for the third reading. Early in the new year, Edward Taylor wrote to the chief whip expressing the view that 'we must weigh well how the absentees from one or both [divisions] should be treated – I am for a remonstrance in some shape – otherwise calculation is impossible & our whipping labours are completely thrown away', but he acknowledged that 'we must be careful not to affront & so alienate completely those who declined voting'. George Hamilton, on the other hand, doubted the wisdom even of a remonstrance, thinking that 'it won't do to complain or to scold them', and his view seems to have prevailed.[10]

Of course, there is no intention of suggesting that the ties between MPs and their parties were unimportant. Loyalty to the party leader was one obvious and powerful constraint upon the conduct of MPs, and even in opposition, when, as George Hamilton put it, 'the bonds of party have always a tendency to become slackened', he doubted whether 'the allegiance of any of his party to Lord Derby, if called forth by his personal influence, would be found wanting'.[11] Underlying such loyalty was a common commitment to certain policy objectives, and, possibly, a fear of offending constituents by a too-blatantly wayward course. The only other hold that the party managers had over back-benchers was the prospect of access to sources of patronage when their party was in office. While the distribution of patronage as a political lubricant is normally associated with the eighteenth century, it survived in a modified form throughout the nineteenth century (and beyond). Pensions and sinecures may have become largely a thing of the past by the 1840s, but there was a tremendous expansion of what has been termed 'salaried patronage', especially at the local level, such as appointments in the Post Office and the customs service. Even the porters and messengers in some public buildings were political appointees. Unpaid, but honorific posts, most notably appointments to the magistrates' bench, were also available, and for a fortunate few there might be a knighthood or some other title. Patronage of the kind described was used by MPs as a way of rewarding political supporters and their relatives, and the papers of the party whips are full of requests for assistance to this end. John Tollemache, the member for South Cheshire, made no less than seventy-nine applications for patronage, on behalf of his constituents, between 1841 and 1843.[12] The whips thus had a vital role to play as the conduits for MPs' requests to ministers for honours and employment. There is no evidence of whips systematically withholding patronage from dissident back-benchers – it was hardly in a party's interests to undermine an MP's local position to the extent that he lost his seat – but it must have been clear to the average MP that it was desirable to keep on good terms with his whip: the implicit threat of no carrot, rather than a stick, was what enabled the whips to exercise some control over their 'flocks'.

The whips could be of great service to the back-bencher in other respects, too. Advice might be sought as to when an MP's presence was likely to be required for an important division, and, if his absence was unavoidable, a 'pair' could often be arranged. 'Pairing' meant that two MPs of opposite parties agreed to absent themselves from a specific division, or for a specified period of time, so that their votes were cancelled out.[13] It was common for the whips to arrange for MPs to pair off for the 'dinner hour', which in fact lasted from 7 till 10 p.m. (when divisions were not expected to take place), or to pair them for the whole evening if required. This serves to highlight the important point that the life of Parliament, which was usually only in session from February until July or August, was integrally related to the wider social life of London, with its salons and clubs, dinners and balls, and that the majority of MPs, who were not professional politicians, expected to be able to mix their senatorial obligations with a fair – or more than fair – amount of pleasure. Pairing arrangements were, of course, 'gentleman's agreements', and the successful operation of the system required a degree of trust between the whips of opposing parties, which usually seems to have existed. Only rarely do we find the sort of expressions of distrust contained in a letter to the Conservative chief whip, prior to the 1839 session, warning him of his Liberal counterpart:

The Government are obviously very uneasy as to their position, and I strongly suspect that they are aware of their danger from the *absence* rather than the *opposition* of many of their old supporters . . . I need not say that [E. J.] Stanley is not scrupulous and might use names for pairing *without express authority* tho' once done they might hesitate to annul his act.

I should therefore *most strongly urge you* to decline *all* such negotiation with him *for the next ten days or a fortnight* . . . You will then have . . . ample time for any *legitimate* pairs, and *also* for some inquiry into those he may propose.[14]

For a chief whip to be fully effective it was essential for him to establish a confidential relationship with his leader, because there were so many delicate matters to be dealt with, quite apart from the routine business of managing the parliamentary party. Whips were involved, for instance, in the discussions surrounding the formation of a ministry, where it was clearly important to achieve a balance between the claims of contending sections of the party, and to try to satisfy the ambitions of individuals, some of whom could prove dangerous if left out. This can be illustrated by the case of Earl Russell's Liberal government, formed after the death of Palmerston in October 1865. It was felt that the behaviour of a former office holder, who had been particularly troublesome to Palmerston's ministry after resigning his office, made him unacceptable as a colleague, while another maverick was not recruited because Russell was unwilling to make him a sufficiently tempting offer. But a high price was paid for the exclusion of Edward Horsman and Robert Lowe, who became two of the key figures in the revolt of the 'Adullamites', which brought down the government in June 1866.[15] One way in which a government could confer a mark of favour on its back-bench followers was to invite two of them to move and second the Address, following the Queen's speech at the opening of Parliament, but the selection of suitable candidates could raise all sorts of tricky problems, such as 'whether it would be according to Parliamentary etiquette for a County member to second, where a Borough member proposes' – the status and dignity of a knight of the shire being considered greater than that of a mere borough representative.[16] Much worse still was the task of determining which MPs should be awarded more tangible honours in the form of titles, something to which many an ordinary back-bencher

aspired as the only feasible climax to his political career. Distributing honours was a notoriously difficult and often unpleasant
business, because of the jealousy it aroused among those members who were not favoured with an award. Certain other practical considerations also had to be borne in mind, and so, for
example, the Conservative MP Sir Henry Selwin Ibbetson, proposed for a peerage in 1889, had to wait until the dissolution of
Parliament in 1892, in order to avoid an unnecessary by-election
in his Essex constituency which would have been extremely in-
convenient to an unpopular government in mid-term.[17] On one
occasion, this same Conservative government had an unwanted
vacancy forced upon it when the disgruntled member for the
Wisbech division of Cambridgeshire, who felt that the £13,000 he
had spent on the constituency entitled him to a baronetcy, threatened to resign his seat in protest at not being so honoured: the
chief whip took the view that it was impossible to yield to such
pressure, the threat of resignation was carried out, and the seat
lost at the ensuing by-election.[18] A trusted whip might also carry
out exceptionally discreet assignments for his leader, as in the case
of Lord Richard Grosvenor, during Gladstone's second administration (1880–85), who maintained a secret line of communication with the Irish Nationalist leader, Charles Stewart Parnell,
through Parnell's mistress, Katharine O'Shea, at a time when it
would have been impossible for the government to be publicly
seen to be consulting with the Nationalists.[19]

An interesting case-study of a chief whip at work, in delicate
political circumstances, is provided by W. P. Adam,[20] who was
in charge of Liberal management in January 1875 when Gladstone
stunned his followers by announcing that he was resigning as
leader. The Liberals had been in opposition since suffering a
devastating election defeat early in 1874, and Gladstone's resignation therefore raised the practical question of who should assume the leadership of the party in the House of Commons (Lord
Granville continuing to lead the peers), since this was not a matter
for the royal prerogative, and there was no established procedure
for electing a leader. Granville, and most of his fellow ex-Cabinet
colleagues, regarded Lord Hartington, the heir of the Duke of
Devonshire and thus a young representative of the 'Whig' tradition of aristocratic leadership, as the best man to fill Gladstone's
place, and it is possible that if nature had been left to take its

course Hartington would have gradually 'emerged' as the new Commons' leader, without this ever being formally ratified by the party. However, a number of 'independent' MPs, on the left of the party, were anxious not to allow the leadership question to be settled by default, and, in order to improve the chances of their preferred candidate, W. E. Forster, they sent a requisition to the chief whip calling for a meeting of the party to be summoned.[21] Adam felt obliged to respond to this request, but it opened up the alarming prospect of a damaging public contest between rival sections of the Liberal Party. His own impression was that Hartington was more likely than Forster to be able to unite the Liberals, Forster's reputation having been damaged by his handling of the controversial Education Act of 1870, which had angered much of the nonconformist element within the party, but the problem was that few MPs were in London in January for their opinions to be canvassed. 'The only thing to be done now', Adam reported to Granville, 'is to ascertain as far as we can the real feelings of the party so that the matter may if possible be settled without an actual division.' In the opinion of Lord Cardwell, an ex-Cabinet Minister, the crucial question was 'will Adam be able to find out what the party wishes before it meets? or will the gates be opened, when it meets, for a general outpouring of rivalries and dislikes? A great deal, I think, may depend on what Adam may be able to accomplish in this respect. Otherwise, everyone may be damaged, and no one chosen'.[22] Accordingly, Adam spent late January in gathering the written opinions of as many MPs as he could possibly contact, many of whom were unable or unwilling to come up to London for the party meeting, and the result of his efforts showed a small majority in favour of Hartington, confirming the original view of Granville and others that Forster would be a liability as leader.[23] This, along with public demonstrations of continued nonconformist hostility, persuaded Forster that his leadership was an impossibility, and he therefore announced that he would not be seeking the position. The Liberal Party meeting went ahead at the Reform Club on 3 February, with the veteran radical, John Bright, presiding (at Adam's suggestion), but as there was no contest, nothing remained to be done but to endorse Hartington as the new leader.

A second case-study, which also exemplifies the vital,

constructive role which the whips sometimes played as liaison officers between the front and back benches, relates to the Conservative Party managers of the 1850s. This was a particularly testing time for the Conservatives, who were in opposition for most of the decade, as the Crimean War of 1854–56, and the emergence of Palmerston as Liberal Prime Minister, made it hazardous for them to engage in attacks on the government without appearing factious and unpatriotic. Even after the war was over, it often seemed to the Conservative whips that the party had no alternative but to adopt a cautious policy of wait and see, such was the popularity of Palmerston (see Doc. 20). The situation was further complicated by the fact that the Earl of Derby, the acknowledged overall leader, sat in the House of Lords, and relied on his lieutenant, Disraeli, to lead the party in the Commons. Disraeli, however, was still the object of deep distrust on the part of many Conservative MPs, who regarded him as an unprincipled adventurer of dubious social origins.[24] Furthermore, he aggravated an already difficult set of circumstances by his personal aloofness, and unwillingness to consult with his colleagues and back-bench followers. With Derby himself prone to long periods of inactivity (partly because he suffered badly from attacks of gout), the state of the Conservative Party was at times a cause of serious concern to the whips, as is illustrated by a frantic letter from Edward Taylor to Sir William Jolliffe, in November 1856:

> if we could only get Ld Derby to show the least disposition of intent in the holding together of the party, I should have hopes still – but if he continues to hold aloof, does nothing, & communicates with nobody, it is only natural that many of our best men should complain, & finding no redress, & receiving no explanations should ride off on their own hobbies.[25]

George Hamilton confirmed that the impression often given by Derby of indifference to politics was having a damaging effect on Conservative morale, and he also reported that the spectacle of front-bench Conservatives in the House of Commons taking an independent line on issues such as national education and the Maynooth grant, on which many back-benchers held strongly contrary opinions, had contributed to the demoralised condition of the party. Significantly, he observed that 'when this

kind of dissatisfaction prevails, arising from want of unanimity in opinion among the leaders themselves – & between the leaders & followers – the disadvantages which appertain to Disraeli are brought more prominently forward. People say "no one trusts D" . . . which never wd arise if there was a proper understanding between leaders and followers'.[26] The response to these complaints is of considerable interest, for Jolliffe attended a private meeting with Derby and another leading Conservative peer, Lord Malmesbury, as a result of which Derby promised to take action in order to stop the rot. Several of the more prominent frontbench dissidents were invited to Derby's country seat at Knowsley for consultations, and arrangements were made for regular meetings of the opposition leadership to be held during the forthcoming parliamentary session. Hamilton, for one, welcomed this outcome as laying the foundations for co-ordinated action by the party, which would therefore be in 'a better state of preparation in the event of any crisis'.[27] This enhanced level of organisation was only to be a temporary phenomenon, but it is intriguing to speculate as to what contribution it may have made to the defeat inflicted on Palmerston's government in March 1857, when a 'crisis' did suddenly arise over the China War.

Far from being the dictatorial figures of political legend, it can be argued that the whips performed an invaluable service for the ordinary back-bencher as well as for the party leaders. Their task was often a thankless and unpleasant one: 'We shall have to endure endless torture', was the consoling way in which Taylor greeted the news that the 1860 session of Parliament was to be summoned early.[28] One junior whip on the Liberal side, Edward Knatchbull Hugessen, complained that his job was 'one which sometimes brings me into unpleasant contact with members who are apt to treat the "whips" as if they were an inferior order of being'.[29] It was certainly the case that for most of the nineteenth century, a spell in the whips' office offered little prospect of political promotion. Some chief whips such as the Liberal, Henry Tufnell (1841–50), went unrewarded for their labours, while William Hayter (1850–59) only received a baronetcy. Among the Conservatives, Jolliffe (1853–60), did eventually receive a peerage, but his successor, Taylor (1860–68), though given a junior post in Disraeli's governments, was bitterly disappointed at not being made a peer. Two Liberal chief whips, Henry Brand

(1859–67) and Arthur Peel (1873–74), went on to become Speakers of the House of Commons, while W. P. Adam (1874–80) was appointed Governor of Madras, though he died soon after arriving in India. The typical Victorian whip, of either party, was a respectable country gentleman, closely attuned to the values and attitudes of those whom he sought to organise, and it may have been an advantage if he was not perceived to be acting from a desire for personal aggrandisement. Not until the 1880s, by which time politics was becoming rather more of a game for professionals, were there signs of change in the social character of the whips and in their career prospects. Liberals like Arnold Morley (1886–92), the son of a Nonconformist manufacturer, and Tom Ellis (1894–99), the rising star of Welsh Liberalism, were not recruited from the old charmed circle, while on the Conservative side, Aretas Akers Douglas (1885–95), archetypal Kentish gentleman though he may have been, was later appointed Home Secretary.[30] At the end of our period, then, a new pattern was beginning to emerge, later to become well-established, in which the post of whip carried considerably greater authority, and the chances it afforded for political advancement increased commensurately.

******

Turning from the party managers to those whom they sought to manage, it should now be clear that the Victorian back-bench MP was often a great deal more than 'lobby fodder' at the command of the whips. It remains for us to explore the world of the private member, by considering whether he went into Parliament primarily as the defender of vested interests, and by ascertaining what he could and could not hope to achieve there, both in an independent capacity and as part of a collective entity. We also need to assess the extent to which the position of the private member of Parliament was changing, towards the end of the nineteenth century, as a result of the expanding electorate and consequent constituency pressures.

Superficially, it would be easy to dismiss Parliament as merely an institution that was in the hands of powerful vested interests, and this would appear to be true, above all, of the aristocratic and landed class. Quite apart from the House of Lords, which was an entirely hereditary body except for the bishops, and for membership of which substantial landholdings were almost an

essential precondition, the House of Commons was also dominated, until the 1880s, by men closely connected to the peerage or
to landed society (see chapter 4). And there were certainly radical critics who believed that MPs were too often motivated by a
desire to protect their own class interests. Richard Potter, in the
1830s, observed how on one occasion, when the House was debating the question of whether parochial funds should be used
to pay for the state registration of births, marriages and deaths,
'the Landed interest could not, even in this minute case, conceal
that selfish conduct which generally characterises their proceedings in the House'.[31] A radical MP of a later generation also noted,
for example, the way that the country gentlemen attended in
large numbers, right at the end of the 1862 session, in order to
push through a Night Poaching bill, increasing the powers of
the police, and the way that, several years later, pressure from
landed MPs (including the Speaker of the House of Commons,
John Evelyn Denison) forced the Chancellor of the Exchequer to
abandon plans for new taxes on horses.[32] Evidence of this kind
has to be offset, however, by the glaringly obvious fact that this
same body was unable to prevent the repeal of the Corn Laws in
1846, partly because of outside pressure orchestrated by the Anti-
Corn Law League, but also, crucially, because a significant number
of landed MPs (and also peers) had been converted to the general
principle of Free Trade. Indeed, by 1852 even the leaders of the
protectionist Conservatives, Derby and Disraeli, had abandoned
the idea of trying to restore the Corn Laws. Thereafter, no
Victorian government, not even Lord Salisbury's Conservative
ministries which dominated the political scene in the last fifteen
years of the century, dared to challenge the prevailing Free Trade
orthodoxy. That this was so is all the more remarkable when
we recall the serious damage done to British agriculture, from
the 1870s onwards, by cheap imports of foodstuffs. Only in the
Edwardian period did it seem possible that agricultural protection might return, but this was a relatively minor aspect of
Joseph Chamberlain's imperially-inspired campaign for Tariff
Reform.

A similar picture emerges when we examine what may be
regarded as an ancillary branch of the aristocratic and landed
interest, represented by those MPs with connections to the armed
services. In every Parliament up to 1880 there was a large body

of current or former military officers, sometimes including as many as 100 army men, and, typically, about a dozen from the navy. There was always a preponderance of Conservatives amongst the military men, but it was only after 1885 that this bias became overwhelming.[33] Frequent complaints were again made by radicals that army and navy officers took unfair advantage of their seats in the House of Commons in order to further their material interests, often in very petty ways.[34] But when it came to a major measure of reform like the Army Regulation bill of 1871, which abolished the system whereby commissions in the army were purchased, the vehement opposition and deliberate obstructionist tactics of the 'Tory Colonels', backed up by strong resistance in the House of Lords, were not enough to stop a determined government from imposing its policy.

Important business interests also had a considerable presence in the House of Commons during the Victorian period, but they were never in a position where they could dominate proceedings and coerce governments. The railway industry, which grew rapidly in Britain from the 1830s onwards, had the potential to become a formidable interest group because of the trend towards large-scale company organisation through amalgamations, and because large numbers of MPs sat on the boards of directors of these companies. And yet, in November 1868, we find the *Railway Times* complaining that:

> There were, in the House of Commons during 1868, no less than 158 directors, few of whom, however, took any great interest in its [the railway lobby's] general claims for protection or consideration. Many were careless, others lukewarm, both retreating under the plea that they had not been sent to Parliament as guardians of railway proprietaries.[35]

In reality, there was a group of between thirty and forty MPs, in each late-Victorian Parliament, associated with the major railway companies, who constituted the efficient strength of the railway interest. Many belonged to the parliamentary sub-committee of the Railway Companies Association (1867). The work of the railway interest was conducted largely behind the scenes, rather than on the floor of the House of Commons, for instance through participation on the various select committees appointed to inquire into the industry or to scrutinise bills affecting it. After

1886, the majority of railway MPs were Conservatives, and the industry's relations were much more cordial with Conservative than with Liberal administrations, but even so three out of the five major pieces of legislation regulating the railways, passed between 1886 and 1900, were the work of Conservative governments. The railway interest undoubtedly had the power to influence the details of legislation, but the industry was never immune from the tendency towards greater state interference in its affairs.

Another industry characterised by its large-scale company organisation was brewing, and, particularly during the later decades of the nineteenth century, the drink interest (often known simply as 'the trade') acquired a sinister reputation for wielding immense political influence and even bringing down governments.[36] Many of the more hysterical accusations made against 'the trade', it has to be said, originated from temperance campaigners alarmed by the rapid growth in per capita alcohol consumption during the mid-Victorian years. In parliamentary terms, the truth of the matter was that there were about a dozen MPs, in each Parliament from 1832 to 1859 inclusive, who were either brewers or were involved in related businesses (distillers, hop merchants, wine merchants, etc.). This figure rose to between twenty and thirty MPs per Parliament in the 1865–85 period, and briefly reached a climax of fifty in the Parliament of 1886–92, before going into decline. As in the case of those MPs connected with railway companies, members representing 'the trade' did not act as a monolithic political bloc. An analysis of twenty-one major parliamentary divisions affecting the drink industry in the years 1871–1914, including proposals for the Sunday closing of public houses, and for the outright prohibition of the sale of alcohol, shows that only about one-half of the MPs nominally attached to 'the trade' could be relied on to vote against temperance measures, while many simply did not bother to attend, and a few even supported certain temperance reforms. The lack of political cohesion amongst MPs reflected the sectionalised nature of the industry in the country, where the London-based brewers were disdainful of their provincial counterparts in centres like Burton-on-Trent and Manchester, who were in turn very independently minded. Ironically, if by the end of the nineteenth century the threat of state intervention in the drink industry had receded, this was owing less to the political power of 'the trade', as to the fact that, for various social reasons, alcohol consumption was on the decline.

Economic self-interest, then, as an analytical tool, does not take us very far towards an understanding of what happened at Westminster. This point is reinforced when we consider some of the major issues which divided politicians during the Victorian era. In the 1840s, for example, there was considerable controversy surrounding the 'Ten Hours bill' for textile factories, but it has been demonstrated by W. O. Aydelotte that MPs' voting behaviour on this issue was not generally related to their economic and social backgrounds. Thus, aristocratic and landed MPs, on the one hand, and businessmen MPs on the other, voted in roughly the same proportions for and against the bill. Surprising as it may seem, a clear majority of MPs with backgrounds in manufacturing industry *supported* the Ten Hours bill both in 1844 and 1847 (when it finally passed). Curiously, there was much greater opposition to the measure from MPs who were merchants.[37] Careful investigation has also disposed of the old myth that the 'Peelites', those Conservatives who supported the repeal of the Corn Laws, were a more business-oriented group than the protectionist Conservatives. On the contrary, little difference can be detected in the social composition of the Peelites and the Protectionists. J. B. Conacher's analysis of the forty-eight Peelites who survived into the Parliament of 1847–52, shows that only five had been directly involved in business, another five had pursued an active legal career, while the overwhelming majority were 'men of leisure drawn from the landed classes'. Nor did the Peelites differ greatly from the Protectionists in terms of the constituencies they represented, sitting as they did mainly for counties and small boroughs: only eight were elected by boroughs with electorates of over 1,000, and of these only Liverpool, Oldham and Stockport were major industrial or commercial centres.[38] In recent years, another popular assumption which has come under increasing attack is that the Liberal schism of 1886, over the question of Home Rule for Ireland, simply involved a 'revolt of the Whigs', with the Irish Question being used by right-wing Liberals to justify their secession from a party with which they no longer had anything in common. The work of W. C. Lubenow suggests that Liberal MPs from aristocratic and landed backgrounds were only slightly more likely than other Liberals to oppose Gladstone's Irish policy, and that the schism cannot be explained by reference to other factors like the age of MPs or the type of constituency they represented.[39]

Many reasons could be put forward to explain why MPs often did not act from a sense of 'class interest', such as the fact that aristocrats and landowners often had subsidiary business interests, or that businessmen sometimes aspired to be assimilated into the old social elite by purchasing a landed estate, or perhaps that constituency pressures overrode economic self-interest. One other possibility, which is worth exploring in some depth, is that the House of Commons possessed a communal identity which could do much to condition the attitudes of its members, encouraging a broader view of the national interest. MPs, that is to say, were not merely social atoms, but also part of a greater organism with its own distinct character.

Political observers like the radical journalist, E. M. Whitty, emphasised how important it was for newly-elected Members of Parliament to acclimatise themselves to the atmosphere of the House of Commons, which was not something that could be breathed by outsiders relying on newspaper reports of proceedings. 'The House is a great theatre, with its green-room as well as its stage. It is a great club, all in all, in itself and to itself, with its own heroes, its own way of thought, and its own way of talk.'[40] Interestingly, Whitty accepted that though the Commons was of course a very aristocratic body, given its personnel, social status was by itself no guarantee that a member would establish a reputation, which depended ultimately on a man's abilities. Reputations made outside the House cut little ice inside, unless justified by members' performance in the chamber, and some were never able to command the attention they might have expected. The hostile reception initially accorded to the flamboyant literary personality, Benjamin Disraeli, is well known, though he at least managed to retrieve his position: George Hudson, the 'railway King', on the other hand, was always laughed and jeered at.[41] During the course of a debate, the chamber would fill, and empty, and fill again, depending on who was speaking. Telegraph messages were sent out to the London clubs when a star performer like Ralph Bernal Osborne, renowned for his jesting style, rose to speak; but a man who was judged to be a 'bore' would probably be drowned out by a cacophony of hisses and coughs and background conversation.[42] Not surprisingly, the sporting instinct was very strong amongst MPs, and the sponsor of a private member's bill, or a vulnerable minister, might well find himself treated as a 'bag fox' for an evening, to provide his brethren with some entertainment. Betting on the outcome of a major division was not unknown.[43] But the same instincts meant that the House appreciated a hard-hitting performance from anyone, even when, as in the case of the radical orator, John Bright, his admiring listeners on the Conservative benches were also his targets.[44]

The qualities that made a man a successful parliamentary speaker cannot very easily be described or analysed with the printed word, and in any case it was partly an individual matter. Palmerston, who dominated the House of Commons during the last decade of his life (1855–65), was not in any conventional sense a great speaker at all, but he possessed a remarkable ability to express the general feeling of the House, usually in a good-natured way.[45] In the Parliament of 1886–92, it was argued that the radical-turned-Liberal Unionist, Joseph Chamberlain, had established himself as the outstanding *debater*, thanks to his 'lightning-like acuteness and consummate gift of lucid expression', resembling a fencer 'warding off bludgeon blows with deft parrying of his rapier, swiftly followed up by telling thrust at the aggressor', but that Gladstone was still the supreme *orator*, with his powerful and impassioned set-speeches.[46] For an ordinary back-bencher, trying to make his mark in the House, the diaries of Sir John Trelawny suggest that the golden rule was to convey an impression of personal modesty to one's hearers, and avoid the appearance of over-confidence, which was likely to cause irritation. Trelawny thus contrasted the 'good, quiet, firm & self-possessed manner' of one member, with another who was 'far too egotistic & personal'.[47] Lawyers had to be especially careful, as the style of advocacy suited to the courts did not go down well in the House of Commons, which 'has a manner of its own and likes it'.[48]

In an unpublished essay written in 1857, Lord Stanley, the son of the Earl of Derby, made a number of practical observations about mastering the technique of debate, 'without which ... nothing more than a second-rate reputation can ever be made in Parlt.' His remarks about preparing oneself for a speech are of particular interest, and in what follows it should be borne in mind that it was considered unacceptable for an MP to read from a script:

> Never divide a speech formally into heads, which looks lawyerlike and pedantic: but have the divisions well marked out in your own mind.
>
> Prepared passages, meant to be effective, are dangerous: if you must use them, it is good to hesitate a little, as though seeking for a word, while you are really repeating from memory . . .
>
> If unpractised, be prepared with a conclusion, in case of failure, arising out of sudden embarrassment.

Stanley recorded a number of other handy 'tricks of the trade'. For instance, if one was replying to speeches from the other side, his advice was to 'speak after someone who has wearied his audience: any change then becomes a relief to the hearers', though he cautioned that 'this should not be attempted at too late an hour', when members were anxious for the division to take place. It was important, in Stanley's opinion, to stick to broad principles rather than concentrating on points of detail, as 'Your object is not to show ingenuity but judgment. It is in proportion as men seem to possess that quality that they are respected in the H. of C'. In many cases, opportunities would arise to undermine the opposing case by pointing out contradictions in the arguments used by the various speakers; it might also be possible to take advantage if any of the opposing speakers overstated their case, by presenting that man's opinions as the real, but suppressed opinions of the others; and ulterior motives could be suggested, even when a proposition was unobjectionable in itself. Furthermore:

> Much may be done by widening or narrowing a subject as suits your interest: as for instance, if defending an abuse, show that it forms part of a system, which on the whole is good, and which will be destroyed by its removal. If arguing the other way, keep these results out of sight, and dwell merely on the actual bad working of which you condemn.

Finally, Stanley warned that one should never persist in trying to speak if it was clear that the House was not disposed to listen, as this was likely to cause offence. It had always to be remembered that 'the H. of C. constitutes a world of its own ... and listens only to those who can amuse or instruct it'.[49]

MPs who were prepared to dedicate themselves to the detailed routine of parliamentary business were always appreciated in the House, though, being cynical, one suspects that this was because so many members were anxious not to undertake such work. E. M. Whitty, writing in the early 1850s, noted that the tenacious advocate of economy in government expenditure, Joseph Hume, who attended Commons debates assiduously, was popular on all sides, whereas his fellow radical, Richard Cobden, who had been a prominent figure in the extra-parliamentary campaign by the Anti-Corn Law League (1838–46), made much less of an impact as he was not regarded as a true parliamentarian.[50] Lord Stanley, in his essay on the position of the Member of Parliament, mentioned several ways in which a man might create an impression in the House of Commons (see Doc. 5), but the approach that he chose for himself was to build up a reputation as a 'man of business'. This involved more than simply regular attendance at debates and in divisions, for the man of business was equally in his element sitting on the numerous select committees which were routinely appointed to scrutinise private bills, such as those concerning railway companies. Membership of private bill committees was 'exceedingly disliked' by the majority of MPs, and so willingness to serve on them naturally enhanced a man's popularity. The man of business also sat on other select committees, set up to inquire into some aspect of public policy, or on Royal Commissions, which had a similar function but whose membership was not confined to Members of Parliament. Through work of this kind, it was possible to acquire a wide range of expert knowledge which could be of use in parliamentary debates, and the man of business might also demonstrate his expertise by publishing pamphlets, preferably in anticipation of an important debate, when his labours might provide other members with source material for their speeches.[51]

Another way in which back-benchers might seek to make their mark in the House of Commons was by introducing a motion in favour of some principle or policy, or else by embodying it in the form of a private member's bill. Such motions and bills were favourite devices of radical MPs, some of whom became identified with particular causes and often acted on behalf of outside pressure groups. C. P. Villiers' annual motions calling for the repeal of the Corn Laws, backed up by the Anti-Corn Law League's extra-parliamentary agitation, are a famous illustration of this phenomenon. The Liberation Society, a prominent non-conformist pressure group, sponsored a bill to abolish Church Rates which was introduced on an almost annual basis, between 1854 and 1863, first by Sir William Clay and later by Sir John Trelawny. In the 1870s, Edward Miall, one of the Liberation Society's leaders, pressed as an MP for the organisation's ulti-mate objective, the disestablishment of the Church of England, and in the same decade George Osborne Morgan, also acting for the Society, brought in an annual Burials bill, designed to allow nonconformist burial services in Anglican cemeteries. From the early 1860s until the end of the century, the foremost advocate of temperance reform in the House of Commons was Sir Wilfrid Lawson, who was associated with the most powerful pressure group in this field, the United Kingdom Alliance.[52] The passing of the second Reform Act, in 1867, which increased the power of the large boroughs and the working-class electors, provided the impetus for more action by MPs to promote legislation of a less ambitious kind, intended to improve the welfare of the peo-ple in practical ways. Whereas in 1864 a total of sixty-six private members' bills were introduced, by 1869 this had risen to eighty-two, and by 1873 it had reached 113, and those which success-fully passed into law included Jacob Bright's Married Women's Property Act (1870), Lubbock's Bank Holiday Act (1871), and Muntz and Dixon's Adulteration of Food and Drugs Act (1872). Much of this legislative achievement was the work of a new gen-eration of MPs representing the large boroughs, typically non-conformist businessmen, who did not share the distrust of state intervention characteristic of the previous generation of radicals.[53]

There were also occasions when MPs could operate with some effect as members of a parliamentary group. Sometimes, the object was to protect the interests of their constituents, as in the early 1860s when the MPs representing Lancashire, Liberal and Con-servative, worked together to obtain relief for their county at a time when it was suffering from the cotton famine caused by the American Civil War.[54] In the early 1870s, we find the Cornish county Members (all of whom happened to be Liberals) work-ing closely with the Liberal government in respect of a Mines

Inspection bill affecting their county, to the extent even of helping with the drafting of the bill.[55] Similar group action could be designed to promote a particular cause. For instance, during the sessions of 1871 and 1872 a considerable number of Liberal and Conservative MPs acted together, and in conjunction with leading members of the medical profession, in order to defend the Contagious Diseases Acts, which enforced the inspection of prostitutes working in specified garrison towns and were regarded as vital public health measures. This inter-party group was strong enough both to block private members' initiatives aimed at the repeal of the Acts (the repealers, it might be noted, also straddled the party divide), and to organise a deputation to the Home Secretary which led the Gladstone ministry to drop its own plans for repeal.[56] On the Liberal back-benches, in the early 1880s, there briefly emerged a group known as the 'Young Whig Party', who were alarmed by the implications of the Irish Land legislation introduced by Gladstone's second ministry, and they made a strong enough showing in the division lobbies to force the Prime Minister to make concessions in his Land bill of 1881 (see Doc. 25).[57] Attempts were also made by MPs representing the 'Celtic fringe' to organise themselves as a means of furthering their national interests. The increasingly well-disciplined Irish Nationalist party of the 1880s provided a model in this respect: early in 1886, the Scottish Liberal members met to consider forming their own party, though they decided in favour of regular consultation only, and the subsequent Irish Home Rule crisis caused a disastrous split in their ranks; but the Welsh Liberals, who were hardly affected by the Home Rule crisis, were able to operate as a party within a party, in the late 1880s and 1890s, and succeeded in getting Welsh Church disestablishment placed firmly on the Liberal agenda.[58]

It would be misleading, however, to suggest that there was ever a golden age of the private Member of Parliament, of the sort imagined by Richard Crossman in the 1960s. Crossman believed that during the mid-Victorian period, prior to the 1867 Reform Act, Britain had enjoyed an epoch of classical parliamentary government, in which a system of moderate rule was ensured thanks to the efforts of 'the majority of solid, sensible independent MPs'.[59] There are obvious objections to this view, prompted by our discussion of party development in chapter 2, which showed that almost all MPs were affiliated to one or other of the parties, in spite of their rhetoric of 'independence'. More damaging still to Crossman's thesis is the point that the strongest assertions of independence, in the mid-Victorian House of Commons, came not from the moderate majority, but from those at the extreme ends of the political spectrum, notably the radicals.[60]

The fate of private members' bills, many of them the work of independently-minded radicals, provides a good indication of the limits that generally applied to what back-bench members could achieve by themselves. It was in fact extremely rare for a private members' bill to pass through all its stages, in both House of Parliament, unless the government was prepared to assist it. Without ministerial support, a back-bencher was likely to struggle to obtain sufficient parliamentary time for his bill, and on Wednesdays, the day designated for private members' legislation, there was always a danger that contentious proposals would be 'talked out', by opponents making lengthy speeches until the time limit for Wednesday debates (a quarter to six) was reached.[61] It was not unknown for governments to organise a 'count out', instructing MPs to leave the chamber until their number fell below the quorum of forty, when a motion to adjourn the sitting could be moved.[62] In those cases where major measures of reform were finally enacted, often after many years of pressure from back-benchers, this was usually because a government had been persuaded to adopt the measure as its own. Thus, the bill to introduce a secret ballot for parliamentary elections was brought in on a regular basis over a period of nearly forty years, before Gladstone's ministry passed it in 1872, while the abolition of church rates and the Burials bill, both the subjects of extra-parliamentary campaigns and numerous private members' bills, similarly succeeded only after they became government measures.

We should be equally sceptical of the corollary to the idea of a golden age of the private member, which is that in the later decades of the nineteenth century the growth of party organisation in the constituencies ('the caucus'), necessitated by the expansion of the electorate, resulted in MPs being deprived of their independence. The claim that MPs were being enslaved by the caucus was first made by the Polish writer Moisei Ostrogorski, whose book, *Democracy and the Organisation of Political Parties,* first appeared in an English translation in 1902. According to Ostrogorski, the fact that MPs were being made answerable to their constituency associations meant that there was increasing pressure on them to conform to the orthodox party line, and expressions of defiant independence therefore became too dangerous to be contemplated. Consequently, there was a marked deterioration in the quality of Members of Parliament, as the caucus had created a political environment in which the only people likely to secure election were 'mediocrities', willing to subordinate their own opinions to the dictates of the party machine.[63] In support of his thesis, Ostrogorski referred to two celebrated cases in which prominent radical politicians, W. E. Forster (at Bradford) and Joseph Cowen (at Newcastle), became embroiled in lengthy and acrimonious disputes with local Liberal caucuses whose authority the MPs refused to recognise.

Any attempt at a qualitative comparison of mid and late-Victorian MPs would clearly be extremely hazardous, but there are at least strong grounds for doubting the validity of Ostrogorski's analysis. Neither Forster nor Cowen, for a start, was ever ousted by his local caucus. And even if we accept that the growth of constituency organisations *tended* to impose constraints upon MPs' conduct, we still need to remember that such organisations were primarily a phenomenon of the big cities, and did not exist everywhere. No doubt this helps to explain why the Liberal Party of the 1890s seems to have had at least its usual share of crotchety radicals, like Henry Labouchere (Northampton), Sir Wilfrid Lawson (Cumberland) and Charles Conybeare (Cornwall), whose political virtues may have been many, but certainly did not include blind loyalty to their party leaders. Greater accountability to constituents (whether or not a caucus existed) also explains the high level of MPs' participation in parliamentary proceedings, in terms of speaking and voting, in the final decades of the nineteenth century.[64] By contrast, one has to ask what sort of golden age of the private member it was when, in the 1854 session, 342 out of 646 MPs did not open their mouths once, or when, as in the 1856 session, only one MP voted in all 198 divisions, fifteen missed up to fifty divisions, another seventy-nine were absent from up to 100 divisions, 551 were absent from over 100 divisions, and seven did not vote at all.[65] The testimony of late-Victorian MPs also weighs against the

claim that the House of Commons was being filled with mediocrities. On the contrary, Thomas Phillips Price, a radical elected
for the first time in 1885, was impressed by the 'marked spirit of
earnestness about this House of Commons, and also of diligence',
which was, naturally, strongest among the 'courageous, energetic, progressive' radical members. From the opposing side of the
House, Sir Richard Temple thought that the general quality of
the MPs sitting in the Parliament of 1886–92 was good, and that
they represented a healthily wide variety of backgrounds.[66]

Furthermore, there is evidence with which to challenge the
assumption that the caucuses in the big cities wanted docile
mediocrities as their representatives in Parliament. The papers of
Dr Lyon Playfair, an eminent scientist and Liberal MP, who was
seeking a new seat in 1885, show that he was pursued by several
large constituencies anxious to have him as their member. Leeds,
Bristol, Sheffield, Birmingham, Dundee, Aberdeen, Paddington
and Lanarkshire were all interested in him.[67] The Blackfriars and
Hutchesontown division of Glasgow was 'extremely anxious to
secure a Gentleman of influence and experience as their candidate', while in West Bristol it was thought that 'You would get
a great many votes from the numerous people who in such a
constituency don't hold very closely to party'.[68] Francis Schnadhorst, the famous Birmingham wirepuller, explained that 'We
have local candidates but we desire to secure a candidate who
will confer distinction upon the town by his connection with it as
Mr [John] Bright has for so many years', and Playfair's being
'less a combative party politician than a reformer of the social
ills of the people' was considered to be a 'recommendation'.[69]
The scramble to catch Playfair was finally won by South Leeds,
but only after he had initially declined their offer, prompting
the following forthright response: 'We are politicians not beggars.
We could have had a man who would have spent £1,000 a year
in the constituency and would have paid all election expenses,
but we preferred to have a man who would confer distinction on
us rather than one who would pauperize us'.[70] The similarity in
the phrasing of the letters from Birmingham and Leeds, both
desiring a man who would 'confer distinction' upon them, is a
particularly striking feature of this correspondence.

******

In many important respects, the experience of the back-bench Member of Parliament changed surprisingly little during the Victorian period. The conditions in which they were required to work were often deemed to be inadequate: there was, for example, insufficient room in the House of Commons to seat every MP at the same time. Richard Potter recorded that on one evening in May 1834, when a division took place on the pension list, 'There were 542 members in the House, it was a very hot night, I was several times obliged to go into the lobby to get a little fresh air. A want of better accommodation for the members was very apparent'. Divine providence might have appeared to intervene when, a few months later, the old Houses of Parliament were engulfed in flames, but the new Palace of Westminster, for all its Gothic magnificence, was still seriously deficient when it came to the mundane matter of facilities for MPs, and complaints continued to be heard about overcrowding.[71] Until the 1860s, the state of the River Thames, which was effectively the sewer for London, could make parliamentary attendance unbearable in a hot summer, as was famously the case during the 'great stink' of 1858. Late night sittings, with divisions taking place at 'three and four o'clock in the morning', were a familiar part of parliamentary life, and added greatly to the already heavy physical burden placed on conscientious MPs.[72] For a dedicated member such as Edward Baines of Leeds, the labours involved in parliamentary attendance, and in satisfying the demands of a large constituency, were considerable in the 1830s (see Doc. 4), and, as the nineteenth century progressed, the expansion of the electorate meant that Baines' experience became the lot of many more MPs. By 1900, a career in Parliament was a much less attractive option than in the past for amateurs, interested primarily in acquiring social status or, if they already had it, in enjoying to the full the pleasures of London high society. MPs still proclaimed their 'independence', and for many this was not untrue in a financial sense (salaries for MPs were not introduced until 1911), but after the redistribution of seats in 1885 no more than a handful of members owed their seats to territorial influence,[73] and for the rest it was impossible to ignore entirely the obligations imposed by constituency feeling. This in turn helped to strengthen the hands of the whips, in inducing back-benchers to follow the party line in the division lobby, though such control was far from absolute. Perhaps the key difference between the 1830s and the 1890s was that the growth in the scale of government activity, and the trend towards partisan opposition, meant that by the end of the century there was nearly always a clear party line for MPs to follow.

Notes

1 William White, *The Inner Life of the House of Commons*, ed. Justin McCarthy, 2 vols. (London, 1897), i, 4–5.

2 *Ibid.*, i, 27.

3 Lord Douro to Sir Thomas Fremantle, 22 May 1838, Fremantle MSS (Bucks RO), D/FR/111/3/31; Quintin Dick to Fremantle, 20 July 1838, *ibid.*, D/FR/111/4/15.

4 Taylor to Jolliffe, 9 January [1856], Hylton MSS (Somerset RO), DD/HY/24/21/17.

5 Taylor to Jolliffe, 19 January [1859], *ibid.*, DD/HY/18/17/23.

6 Taylor to Jolliffe, nd, *ibid.*, DD/HY/24/22/96.

7 Taylor to Jolliffe, 10 January [1854], *ibid.*, DD/HY/24/7/106.

8 Taylor to Jolliffe, nd [July 1854], *ibid.*, DD/HY/24/7/102.

9 Chilston MSS (Kent RO, U564), letters to Aretas Akers Douglas from: G. Finch, 27 March 1887, C211/3; Sir E. Hill, 7 July 1887, C297/1; E. Swetenham, 21 August [1887], C509/4; Lord C. Hamilton, 15 August 1887, C255/3.

10 Taylor to Jolliffe, 10 January [1855], Hylton MSS, DD/HY/24/21/13; Hamilton to Jolliffe, 6 January 1855, *ibid.*, DD/HY/24/9/69. The list of absentees is *ibid.*, DD/HY/24/9/115.

11 Hamilton to Jolliffe, 'Thursday night', nd, *ibid.*, DD/HY/24/7/53.

12 J. M. Bourne, *Patronage and Society in Nineteenth Century England* (London, 1986), pp. 152–5, and chapter 6 generally.

13 MPs could make private pairing arrangements, of course, and these might involve members of the same party if they happened to disagree on the subject at issue.

14 Francis Bonham to Fremantle, 8 February [1839], Fremantle MSS, D/FR/111/2/24.

15 Henry Brand MSS (HLRO), vol. I; J. M. Winter, *Robert Lowe*, (Toronto, 1976), pp. 203–5.

16 Brand to Gladstone, 19 December 1865, BL Add MSS 44193, fo. 132.

17 W. H. Smith to Akers Douglas, 12 October [1889], Chilston MSS, U564/C25/92: – 'bye elections are a bad business for any Government'.

18 Captain Selwyn to Schomberg McDonnell, 14 May 1891, and Akers Douglas to McDonnell, 17 June [1891], Third Marquis of Salisbury MSS

(Hatfield House, Hertfordshire), series E (Akers Douglas letters). McDonnell was Salisbury's private secretary.

19 Grosvenor to Mrs O'Shea, 8 November 1882, 16 March 1883, 21 July 1883, BL Add MSS 44315, fos 94, 114, 123. These letters are in Gladstone's papers.

20 He is reputed to have been the inspiration for the character East in *Tom Brown's Schooldays*.

21 Material relating to this group of MPs survives in the A. J. Mundella MSS, 6P/8, and the Mundella-Leader MSS, 6P/65, both in the Sheffield University Library.

22 Adam to Granville and Cardwell to Granville, both dated 20 January 1875, PRO GD 30/29/28, envelope marked '1875 January-March Leadership Question'.

23 Two bundles of letters with a list, Blairadam MSS (Scottish RO, Edinburgh), 4/413-14. The list gives Hartington a lead of 52 to 46, but three more names should have been added to his total. A number of the replies were very ambivalent.

24 See Robert Stewart, *The Foundation of the Conservative Party, 1830-1867* (London, 1978), pp. 289-97.

25 Taylor to Jolliffe, 25 November [1856], Hylton MSS, DD/HY/24/21/17.

26 Hamilton to Jolliffe, 27 December [1856], *ibid.*, DD/HY/24/11/17.

27 Ibid. Cf. Derby to Jolliffe, 11 January 1857, *ibid.*, DD/HY/18/2/7; Malmesbury to Jolliffe, 13 January 1857, *ibid.*, DD/HY/24/19/3.

28 Taylor to Jolliffe, 9 December [1859], *ibid.*, DD/HY/24/16/1.

29 Diary of Edward Knatchbull Hugessen, 9 August 1860, Brabourne MSS (Kent RO), U951/F27/1.

30 Lord Chilston, *Chief Whip: the Political Life and Times of Aretas Akers Douglas, first Viscount Chilston* (London, 1961).

31 Diary of Richard Potter, 6 June 1836, BLPES, COLL MISC 146.

32 T. A. Jenkins (ed.), *The Parliamentary Diaries of Sir John Trelawny, 1858-1865*, (Royal Historical Society, Camden Fourth Series, vol. 40, 1990), 23-24 July 1862; *The Parliamentary Diaries of Sir John Trelawny, 1868-1873*, (Camden Fifth Series, vol. 3, 1994), 28 May 1869 and 9 June 1870.

33 J. A. Thomas, *The House of Commons 1832-1901: A Study of its Economic and Functional Character* (Cardiff, 1939), pp. 4-5, 14-15.

34 *Trelawny Diaries*, 16 March 1863.

35 Cited by Geoffrey Alderman, *The Railway Interest* (Leicester, 1973), p. 20. I have relied on Alderman's book for the whole of this paragraph.

36 This paragraph is based on David W. Gutzke, 'Rhetoric and Reality: The Political Influence of British Brewers, 1832-1914', *Parliamentary History*, IX (1990), pp. 78-115.

37 W. O. Aydelotte, 'The House of Commons in the 1840s', *History*, XXXIX (1954), pp. 260-2.

38 J. B. Conacher, *The Peelites and the Party System, 1846–52* (Newton Abbot, 1972), pp. 66–68.

39 W. C. Lubenow, 'Irish Home Rule and the Social Basis of the Great Separation in the Liberal Party in 1886', *Historical Journal*, XXVIII (1985), pp. 125–42.

40 E. M. Whitty, *St Stephen's in the Fifties: The Session 1852–3, a Political Retrospect*, ed. Justin McCarthy (London, 1906), p. 2.

41 *Ibid.*, pp. 10–12.

42 *Ibid.*, pp. 41–5, for 'bores'; White, *Inner Life of House of Commons*, i, 90–5, for fluctuating attendance in the chamber.

43 *Trelawny Diaries*, 20 March 1861 and 27 June 1862, for 'bag foxes'. Occasionally a bigger quarry was sought, see 4 June 1863 for a 'Gladstone hunt'. For betting, see 10 June 1859.

44 *Ibid.*, 8 June 1858 and 13 March 1865.

45 White, *Inner Life of House of Commons*, i, 2–4; *Trelawny Diaries*, 7 June 1860 and 7 August 1862.

46 Henry W. Lucy, *A Diary of the Salisbury Parliament, 1886–1892*, (London, 1892), pp. 145–7.

47 *Trelawny Diaries*, 14 April 1864. See also, 24 January and 9 March 1860.

48 *Ibid.*, 25 March 1862 and 6 March 1863.

49 Lord Stanley's essay, 'The Member of Parliament: his position and duties, 1857', Liverpool RO, 920 DER (15) 41/2.

50 Whitty, *St Stephen's in the Fifties*, pp. 6–7.

51 Stanley's essay, 920 DER (15) 41/2.

52 D. A. Hamer, *The Politics of Electoral Pressure* (Brighton, 1977); G. I. T. Machin, *Politics and the Churches in Great Britain, 1832–1921*, 2 vols. (Oxford, 1977–87).

53 Jonathan Parry, *The Rise and Fall of Liberal Government in Victorian Britain* (Yale, 1993), pp. 229–31.

54 J. R. Vincent (ed.), *Disraeli, Derby and the Conservative Party: The Political Journals of Lord Stanley, 1849–69* (Brighton, 1978), p. 185.

55 *Trelawny Diaries*, 16 March, 30 March and 30 May 1870.

56 *Ibid.*, 20 February, 23 March, 11 May, 8–9 July 1872.

57 T. A. Jenkins, *Gladstone, Whiggery and the Liberal Party, 1874–1886* (Oxford, 1988), pp. 141–76.

58 Conor Cruise O'Brien, *Parnell and his Party* (Oxford, 1964); diary of Arthur Elliot, 10 March 1886, NLS MSS 19512; Michael Barker, *Gladstone and Radicalism: The Reconstruction of Liberal Policy in Britain, 1885–94* (Brighton, 1975), pp. 119–25.

59 Walter Bagehot, *The English Constitution*, ed. R. H. S. Crossman (London, 1963), pp. 39–40.

60 Hugh Berrington, 'Partisanship and Dissidence in the Nineteenth Century House of Commons', *Parliamentary Affairs*, XXI (1968), pp. 359–61.

61 *Trelawny Diaries*, 3 July 1872 and 9 July 1873, showing that both sides were guilty of this tactic.

62 *Ibid.*, 11 June 1861.

63 See the extract from Ostrogorski in H. J. Hanham (ed.), *The Nineteenth Century Constitution* (Cambridge, 1969), pp. 206–10.

64 Gary W. Cox, *The Efficient Secret: The Cabinet and the Development of Political Parties in Victorian England* (Cambridge, 1987), pp. 53–4.

65 *Stanley Journals*, pp. 122, 150–1.

66 Diary of Thomas Phillips Price, 26 February and 2 April 1886, HLRO, MSS 113; Sir Richard Temple, *Life in Parliament: Being the Experience of a Member in the House of Commons from 1886 to 1892* (London, 1893), pp. 7–9.

67 Lyon Playfair to his son, 31 May 1885, Playfair MSS (Imperial College, London), 552.

68 William Jack to Playfair, 28 May 1885, *ibid.*, 1106; Lewis Fry to Playfair, 25 May 1885, *ibid.*, 1101.

69 Schnadhorst to Playfair, 23 and 27 May 1885, *ibid.*, 1112–13.

70 J. Gozney to Playfair, 5 June 1885, *ibid.*, 1103.

71 Diary of Richard Potter, 5 May 1834, BLPES, COLL MISC 146; *Trelawny Diaries*, 23 March and 12 May 1869.

72 Diary of Richard Potter, 3 February 1837; *Trelawny Diaries*, 12 July 1860.

73 H. J. Hanham, *Elections and Party Management: Politics in the Time of Disraeli and Gladstone*, 2nd edn. (Brighton, 1978), p. 405, lists twelve seats which were probably still controlled by patrons in the period 1885–1900.

4

Parliamentary reform

The term 'Parliamentary Reform' has a double-meaning which is rather suggestive: it may be taken to denote the reform of Parliament, achieved through changes in the system of election, but it can also be understood as meaning reform of the electoral system *by* Parliament. While popular agitation undoubtedly contributed to the process by which the nineteenth-century Reform bills were carried, reform could never have occurred, as peacefully as it did, without the positive determination of Parliament itself to act. It is the purpose of this chapter to establish what was achieved, in terms of the reform of electoral representation, and to examine the political circumstances which made it possible for Parliament to reform itself without recourse to revolution. In order to do this, it will also be necessary to ascertain the motives of the authors of the various reform plans.

All of the figures cited by historians for the size of the nineteenth-century electorate are *estimates*, but those produced by the civil servant Sir John Lambert, in 1889, have stood the test of time better than most. Lambert calculated the number of voters before and after each of the three Reform Acts:[1]

Table 4.1   *The growth of the electorate in the UK*

Year	England and Wales	Scotland	Ireland
1831	435,391	4,579	75,960
1833	656,337	64,447	92,152
1866	1,054,297	105,494	204,665
1869	1,960,236	235,709	222,450
1883	2,618,453	310,441	224,018
1886	4,380,333	550,831	737,965

It should be noted that separate Reform Acts were passed for England and Wales, for Scotland, and for Ireland,[2] and that Scottish and Irish voting qualifications were more restrictive than those for England and Wales, until the 1884 Act created a uniform qualification based on household suffrage. There is not space here to detail the wide range of franchises that existed within what was an enormously complicated electoral system, and the following summary is therefore necessarily simplified, but it should help to give an impression of the impact made by the three Reform Acts. In England and Wales, the 1832 reforms established a uniform franchise for *boroughs*, applying to householders occupying premises (they did not have to own them) valued at £10 rental per annum, while in the counties several new voting qualifications were added to the traditional 40-shilling freehold franchise. The effect was to increase the proportion of enfranchised adult males from approximately one in seven to one in five. In 1867, household suffrage (meaning that no minimum rental value was set) became the rule in the boroughs, substantially increasing the number of working men who could vote, and in the counties a £12 household franchise was introduced, the overall result being to increase the proportion of enfranchised adult males to one in three. Finally, in 1884, the principle of 'household suffrage' was extended to the counties, a step which benefited not only agricultural labourers, but also groups like miners, quarrymen, potters and some textile workers, living in small industrial communities in the North and the Midlands. Thereafter, around two in three adult males in England and Wales were registered to vote, the proportions in Scotland and Ireland being somewhat lower.

However, the significance of the nineteenth-century Reform Acts cannot be measured solely in terms of the increase in the numbers who possessed the right to vote. Each Act was accompanied by a redistribution of seats which was arguably of at least equal importance to the overall effect of parliamentary reform. This was particularly true in 1832, when the setting of new franchises would have made little difference if the old structure of representation had been retained. As it was, the partial or total disfranchisement of English boroughs with small populations made 144 seats available for redistribution, of which sixty-four were used to create new borough constituencies, including major industrial centres such as Manchester, Birmingham, Sheffield and Leeds, which had previously lacked direct representation in Parliament. The English counties were given an extra sixty-two seats (it is important to remember that, even after 1832, there were more county voters than borough voters), while the remaining seats were allocated to the Celtic fringe. It has been pointed out that one striking consequence of the franchise and redistribution reforms of 1832 was that a far higher proportion of registered electors than in the past actually had the opportunity to cast their votes in *contested* elections, so that there was no repeat of the extraordinary situation in Scotland in 1826, and in Wales in 1830, where not a single elector in those countries was able to exercise his voting rights.[3]

Redistribution figured less prominently in the second reform settlement, in 1867, although fifty-two seats were taken from small boroughs, but following the third Reform Act of 1884 another major redistribution of seats was undertaken. A total of 138 seats were made available for transfer through the wholesale disfranchisement of small boroughs which had survived the earlier reforms, and the representation of the largest towns and cities was at last put on a basis that roughly reflected their population levels: the Greater London area, for instance, now had sixty-two seats instead of twenty-two, while Liverpool increased its representation from three seats to nine, and Birmingham from three to seven. Moreover, the third Reform Act also laid down, as a general rule, that there should be single-member constituencies (previously, most borough and county constituencies had elected two MPs, and sometimes three), and it has been contended that this change contributed to the development of a class-based pattern of voting, as some of the new single-member seats in London, and in provincial centres like Bristol, Leeds and Sheffield, were dominated by the rapidly growing suburban middle classes.[4]

Of the three Reform Acts, there can be little doubt that the success of the first owed the most to extra-parliamentary pressure. A cyclical depression affecting the industrial districts, and rural poverty aggravated by population pressure, both of which were exacerbated by bad harvests and high food prices, served to create disturbed social conditions in many parts of the country during 1830. Public dissatisfaction with what was commonly perceived to be a corrupt and extravagant system of government, which was placing an oppressive burden of taxation on the backs of the people, was given an organisational focus through the spread of the Political Unions, of which nearly 120 can be traced in the period up to the summer of 1832. The most recent study of the Political Unions has stressed the social 'respectability' of their memberships, consisting as they mainly did of skilled working men ('artisans') and the middle classes, and their role seems to have been to provide a safe channel for expressions of political protest.[5] Certainly, when we consider the violent demonstrations that took place when the House of Lords rejected the Reform bill in October 1831, such as the burning of the Bishop of Bristol's palace, it is clear that the potential existed for an extremely dangerous confrontation between the authorities and the mob. The Political Unions, by contrast, provided a comparatively 'legitimate' form of popular pressure, and they succeeded in maintaining the pressure for reform until the issue was finally settled in June 1832. One potent source of inspiration for the extra-parliamentary reform movement was provided by the 'July revolution' in France in 1830, which had demonstrated that a reactionary regime could be replaced by a reformist one without the situation sliding into anarchy.[6]

Parliamentary reform, achieved by due constitutional process, would not have been possible in the early 1830s, however, without a favourable alignment of political forces at Westminster. Earlier agitations for reform, in the 1790s and 1810s, had been suppressed by 'Tory' governments, but in November 1830 a Whig-dominated administration took office, headed by Earl Grey, which was sympathetic to the cause of reform. Ironically, the disintegration of Wellington's Tory government, which paved the way

for Grey and the Whigs, had little to do with parliamentary reform, being primarily the result of violent internal quarrels over
the issue of Catholic Emancipation.[7] By November 1830, in consequence, a number of disaffected 'Liberal Tories', notably
Palmerston and Melbourne, had thrown in their lot with Grey
and the Whigs, and in the process they came to accept the Whig
analysis that a reform bill was urgently required as a palliative
to the social unrest in the country. Not all Whigs, it is true, had
favoured reform prior to 1830, but there had been a growing current of opinion, especially amongst the younger generation such
as Lord John Russell, recognising that if the tradition of government by the aristocracy was to be preserved, it was essential
that the worst defects of the electoral system be removed. The
Whigs therefore sought to devise a franchise and redistribution
package which would dispose of the 'rotten boroughs', where
there was virtually no population to be represented, and to at-
tach to the Constitution those whom the Whigs liked to think
of as the sober, respectable, educated, 'middling classes'.[8] It
has recently been suggested that the Whig ministers regarded
the redistribution of seats, providing direct parliamentary representation for the new industrial centres, as the key to securing
the allegiance of the 'middling classes', rather than the reformed
franchise, since the £10 borough household qualification varied
in its effect from one part of the country to another, according to
local property values, and did not mark a reliable cut-off point
between the middling and the lower classes.[9] What is beyond any
doubt is that the authors of the 1832 Reform Act had no intention
of surrendering political power to the middling classes, but were
attempting to strengthen and sustain the aristocracy's customary
role as the (self-appointed) leaders of the people.

King William IV's role in the reform crisis tends to be over-
looked, but it is arguable that without his initial concurrence
with the Whigs' assessment of the political situation, in November 1830, the Reform bill would never have got off the ground
(see Doc. 6). It was a great stroke of good fortune for the Whigs
that George IV had died the previous June, for his personal hostility to Grey and his friends would have made it extremely difficult for him to accept them as his ministers. At least King William
had no such personal objections to appointing a Whig government. Indeed, his recognition of the need for a settlement of the

reform question made him a valuable ally for the Whigs during the general election of 1831, enabling them to present themselves to the nation as the loyal ministers of the Crown.

It should now be possible to see how the parliamentary and extra-parliamentary dimensions to politics interacted during the early 1830s. In spite of the pressure for action from the Political Unions, it is highly unlikely that a Reform bill would have been introduced but for the fortuitous advent of Grey's government. On the other hand, it is equally unlikely that the Whigs would have proposed such a drastic measure, particularly in its provision for a large-scale redistribution of seats, but for their perception that the turbulent state of the country demanded it. Parliamentary reform was, for the politicians, something of a panacea, a cure for all social ills, and this was why the Whigs felt obliged to prescribe a much larger dose of reform medicine than most would have considered prudent even a couple of years earlier. Furthermore, it is probable that without the political momentum provided by the extra-parliamentary campaign for reform, the Whigs would have been unable to force their bill through Parliament. Even after the general election in the spring of 1831, which produced a decisive majority for reform in the House of Commons, there was still the formidable obstacle of a hostile House of Lords to overcome, and, unless the pressure from beyond Westminster had been maintained, the Whigs' bill would either have foundered completely, or else they would have been compelled to agree to a compromise solution of the kind favoured by King William (who was becoming seriously alarmed by the agitation in the country). Outside pressure thus ensured that the contents of the Reform bill were not watered down: reluctantly the King was forced to give a pledge that he would if necessary create new peers in order to swamp the Tory majority in the House of Lords, at which point the bill was allowed to pass.

The absence of any similar combination of parliamentary and extra-parliamentary pressures for reform helps to account for the fact that, in spite of further rapid industrialisation and urbanisation in Britain, thirty-five years were to elapse before a second bill was finally placed on the statute book. At times of economic hardship, in the late 1830s and 1840s, the Chartist campaign emerged as a focus for working-class discontent, and, in 1839, 1842 and 1848, monster petitions were collected in support of the six points of the 'Charter' – namely, universal suffrage (for men), secret ballot for elections, annual Parliaments, equal elect-oral districts, payment of MPs, and the abolition of the prop-erty qualification for MPs. But there was never any prospect of governments voluntarily yielding to pressure from a movement which, with all its radical implications, was unable to exert much political leverage by gaining support from within the existing, restricted electorate. Since most Chartists were not prepared to adopt the alternative strategy of working for the revolutionary overthrow of the political system, their position was ultimately hopeless. By mid-century, with economic conditions generally improving, Chartism had virtually died out. While it is therefore obviously true that the Chartists achieved nothing in the short term, one important legacy of their campaign was that it placed the question of moderate parliamentary reform back on the political agenda. Lord John Russell, the Liberal Prime Minister from 1846 to 1852, was induced to abandon his position that the 1832 Act was a 'final' measure, and to begin planning a further instalment of reform, while even the Conservative leaders con-templated re-opening the question.[10] Unfortunately for the cause of reform, the relative absence of outside pressure for decisive action, in the 1850s and early 1860s, meant that Russell's new reform proposals foundered on the rocks of apathy and hostile vested interests inside the House of Commons. In 1854 and 1860 Russell introduced bills – the main provisions being for a £10 household franchise in the counties, the reduction of the bor-ough franchise to £6, and a modest redistribution of seats – only to have to abandon them. The Liberal chief whip, Henry Brand, had warned, with respect to the bill of 1860, that there was no possibility of persuading the House of Commons to vote for a reform scheme which would involve the extinction of some MPs' constituencies through redistribution, and which would also require MPs to face the expense of another general election, under the proposed new system, only a year or so after the last election. In any case, Brand argued, there was no chance of MPs agreeing to a reduction in the borough franchise to £6, because of fears among the existing electors that they would be swamped by new working-class voters.[11] The inescapable fact was that, in comparatively quiet times, the parliamentary forces making for legislative inertia were too powerful for Russell to overcome.

In 1866–67, however, an extraordinarily convoluted sequence of events led to the passing of a second, and extensive measure of reform. If we are to make sense of what happened, it is important to bear in mind what has been said about the way circumstances, inside and outside Parliament, served either to facilitate or obstruct the progress of reform. The initial impetus for a renewed effort to deal with that issue came not from extra-parliamentary pressure, in any direct sense, but from the determination of Russell to try his hand once more, when he succeeded to the premiership on the death of Palmerston in October 1865. Russell's chances of success were strengthened by the fact that, while Palmerston himself had always been indifferent to the idea of another reform bill, most other leading Liberals had gradually come round to the view that such a measure was expedient. Above all, the Chancellor of the Exchequer, Gladstone, had become a convert to the reform cause during the early 1860s, seeing a judiciously extended franchise as an appropriate recognition of the growing political maturity of the 'respectable' elements within the working classes, the sort of people who had responded so favourably to his Free Trade policies.[12] Consequently, in 1866, Russell's government introduced a bill which would have given the vote to £14 householders in the counties and £7 householders in the boroughs, and taken forty-nine seats from small boroughs for the purpose of redistribution. In many respects, this bill was more modest than those which Russell had proposed in 1854 and 1860, but the same objections mentioned by the Liberal chief whip in 1860 applied again, as he made clear in a memorandum to Gladstone, prepared after the introduction of the new bill (see Doc. 7). A group of some forty Liberal MPs, known to posterity as the 'Adullamites', were opposed to any reform bill for a mixture of reasons, partly self-interest (some sat for small boroughs scheduled for disfranchisement), and partly a genuine ideological concern about the effects of enfranchising hundreds of thousands of allegedly ignorant and 'venal' working men.[13] In June 1866, the Adullamites joined with the Conservatives in order to defeat Russell's bill, whereupon the government resigned.

It was only after the fall of Russell's government that outside agitation for reform became an element in the political equation, though the crushing of some iron railings and the trampling of a few flowerbeds during the demonstration in Hyde Park in July, organised by the Reform League, was hardly symptomatic of a revolutionary atmosphere. Nor can it be said that such activities were decisive in determining the subsequent course taken by Lord Derby's Conservative ministry, although it undoubtedly helped to confirm the general feeling among the Conservatives that it was desirable to attempt their own settlement of the reform issue. Several months elapsed before any firm decision was taken, but the end result was that during the 1867 session of Parliament Derby's government carried a Reform bill for England and Wales incorporating the principle of household suffrage in the boroughs and a £12 household franchise in the counties. The effects of the Conservatives' measure were considerably more far-reaching than the Liberal plan of 1866: whereas Russell's bill would probably have increased the electorate by about 400,000, the Conservatives added some 900,000, almost doubling the number of voters in England and Wales. Household suffrage was also applied to the Scottish burghs, but in the counties the voting qualification was more restricted than in England and Wales.

When the parliamentary context in which the Conservative government had to operate is taken into consideration, it is easier to see how such a *volte face* on the reform question was possible, indeed necessary. One option for the Conservatives, immediately on taking office in June 1866, was to coalesce with the Adullamites, with whom they had co-operated to defeat Russell's bill, and clearly this would have involved adopting a stance of resolute opposition to any extension of the franchise. Fusion did not take place, however, because the only terms on which leading Adullamites like Lowe and Horsman were prepared to consider it involved Derby and Disraeli being superseded by Derby's son, Lord Stanley, who was one of the most 'liberally' inclined of the Conservatives. The low regard in which Derby held his own son made such an outcome unlikely, quite apart from any other personal considerations.[14] With fusion out of the question, and pressure mounting from many quarters, including the Queen, for the reform issue to be settled, the dilemma for the Conservative leaders was how to respond to this situation given that they did not command a majority in the House of Commons. In June 1866, as in February 1852 and February 1858, Derby had formed a minority administration because of divisions within the ranks

97

of the Liberal majority, and there was an obvious danger that by doing nothing, his third ministry would be as short-lived as the first two. Derby might have attempted to introduce a very moderate reform bill, but it is important to remember that he had done precisely this in 1859, and the result had been to reunite the Liberals in derisive opposition to the Conservatives' plan.[15] If the Conservatives were to find a way of resolving the reform question, and thus gain vital credibility for a party that had been in almost permanent opposition for twenty years, since the Corn Law crisis, there was no alternative but to offer a more radical solution than that proposed by the Liberals. The Conservatives' Reform bill of 1867 therefore adopted the principle of household suffrage for the boroughs, although in practice its operation would have been hampered by the various restrictions that were applied to it. During the bill's progress through the House of Commons, however, these restrictions were either removed or relaxed, in response to pressure from radical Liberal MPs. For instance, the residence requirement before a man could register to vote was reduced from two years to one; a new franchise qualification for lodgers was inserted into the bill, and, most important of all, the government accepted Grosvenor Hodgkinson's amendment which, by abolishing the practice of 'compounding' rent and rates, and so making all householders liable to pay their own rates bill directly, substantially increased the numbers who were eligible to vote. By the time the Reform bill had completed its parliamentary journey, it was a far more radical measure than it had been at its inception.

Disraeli, the Conservative leader in the House of Commons, greatly enhanced his reputation by the skilful way in which he had managed to steer the Reform bill through. Lacking an automatic majority in the Commons for the bill, Disraeli had had to find support for it from somewhere within the ranks of the Liberal opposition. Neither the Adullamites, outraged by the Conservatives' treachery in taking up the reform cause, nor the Liberal leadership, whose own bill had been scuppered by the Conservatives the previous year, were likely to offer a helping hand. This left Disraeli with no option but to bid for the support of radical Liberals who, seeing an opportunity to gain from the Conservatives a more extensive measure than their own leaders were prepared to offer, were willing to support the

Conservatives' bill, provided it was suitably amended. Thus, in the famous 'tea room revolt' of May 1867, some forty-five radicals defied Gladstone by opposing his attempt to insert an amendment to the bill which would have emasculated it. Having passed an extensive Reform bill, the details of which were attributable to parliamentary manoeuvring, it was possible for Disraeli to propagate the myth that the bill was the product of his far-sighted vision of a 'Tory Democracy'. A consideration of much greater importance at the time, however, was that by dealing with the franchise aspect of parliamentary reform, the Conservatives were able to retain control of the accompanying redistribution of seats, which was kept to a minimum. Similarly, the Conservatives had the opportunity to work the re-drawing of constituency boundaries to their own advantage: in particular, they sought to purify the counties (their traditional strongholds) by removing intrusive urban elements whose presence arose from the overspill of towns which had grown beyond the borough boundaries set in 1832.

If extra-parliamentary pressure played a limited role in the reform drama of 1866–67, it was allowed little more than a walk-on part in the 1884 performance. During the 1870s the equalisation of the county and borough franchises, on the basis of household suffrage, became official Liberal policy, and after the party's general election victory in 1880 it was widely anticipated that Gladstone's ministry would introduce a reform bill. After all, the agricultural depression of the late 1870s, caused by cheap foreign competition, was weakening the economic power of many landlords, and to the Liberals it would have seemed that, for the first time, the enfranchisement of agricultural labourers might possibly result in the creation of something other than a homogeneous agrarian block-vote controlled by the landowners. Furthermore, the Liberal government soon found itself in need of a popular measure to help offset the damage done to its reputation by problems in Ireland and elsewhere. A bill to implement household suffrage for the counties was therefore introduced in 1884, and passed by the House of Commons, but the Conservatives used their majority in the Lords to block the measure. Officially, the Conservatives maintained that they had no objection to county franchise reform – at least, they did not wish to be *seen* to be against the policy – but declared that they would not allow the measure to pass until the government brought forward its plan for the redistribution of seats. In effect, Lord Salisbury, the leader of the Conservative peers, was using his party's ability to veto reform, in the upper House, as a bargaining counter with which to obtain some influence over the terms of redistribution. Both Liberal and Conservative party organisations in the constituencies duly responded to the situation with anti- and pro- House of Lords demonstrations during the summer and autumn, but by comparison with the agitation of 1830–32 the whole business was rather tame, and largely synthetic. There is no evidence to suggest that outside pressure had any significant influence on the resolution of the 'crisis', which occurred in November when a small group of Liberal and Conservative leaders met privately at Salisbury's London home, in Arlington Street, and agreed on the details of a redistribution scheme (the 'Arlington Street compact'). The most that can be said is that neither Gladstone nor Salisbury really wished to press the dispute to the point at which a serious 'peers versus the people' agitation *might* have occurred.[16]

Salisbury's motives in November 1884 become clearer when we look at the terms of the deal which he struck with Gladstone.[17] It was on the insistence of the Conservatives that the scale of redistribution was greatly enlarged, so that small boroughs with populations of under 15,000 were swept away altogether, enabling a substantially increased representation to be given to the largest towns and cities. It was also a Conservative demand that the principle of single-member seats be adopted in most places. That Salisbury should have made these his conditions for an agreement, during the Arlington Street negotiations, is indicative of his acute understanding of two vital points: first, that the small boroughs were no longer an electoral asset to the Conservative Party (the Liberals won a majority of such seats in 1880; see Doc. 8), and secondly, that redistribution plus single-member constituencies created an opportunity for the Conservatives to maximise their potential support amongst the 'villa Tories', as Salisbury himself described them, of the suburban areas. Interestingly, at the 1885 general election, the first under the new dispensation, the Conservatives won a majority of English *borough* seats for the first time since before the Great Reform Act, and they were able to consolidate this position at subsequent elections up to 1900.

Two general observations are prompted by this analysis of the nineteenth-century Reform Acts. The first stems from the incremental nature of parliamentary reform. There was in Britain no sudden dash for democracy, of the sort that occurred in certain other European countries, but rather, a gradual absorption of dynamic social classes into the existing constitutional set-up, once it seemed reasonably certain that this could be done without fatally undermining that set-up. In fact, the process of absorption was far from complete even after the 1884 Reform Act, as approximately one-third of adult males in England and Wales, and larger proportions in Scotland and Ireland, were still excluded from the franchise owing to the complexities of the registration rules. Groups such as domestic servants, members of the armed forces living in barracks, and adult males living in their parental home did not qualify as householders, while those who moved house regularly in search of work often found it difficult to satisfy the twelve-month residence requirement which applied before they could register to vote.[18] It has been demonstrated that, during the Edwardian period, the majority of those adult males who were unable to register were unmarried, so that the chief distinguishing feature between enfranchised and unenfranchised males was one of age rather than social class. Many men did not acquire voting rights until they married and established their own households.[19] Women, of course, were completely excluded from the parliamentary franchise until 1918.

The second observation which deserves to be considered is that, from the 1850s onwards, there was an element of competition between the two main political parties in dealing with the reform issue. Thus in 1867 it was possible for a Conservative government to spectacularly outbid the Liberals, when it brought in its own bill, while in 1884 the real question was not whether there should be another extension of the franchise, but what the terms of redistribution should be. From the point of view of the preservation of political stability in Britain, the willingness of both parties to sponsor parliamentary reform, *in certain circumstances*, was clearly of the utmost significance. There was to be no repeat of the dangerous situation in 1830–32, when the country had to choose between a party of reform and a party of resistance to reform.

******

For the remainder of this chapter, our task will be to assess the extent to which the Reform Acts changed the character of politics at the parliamentary level. It might seem a natural assumption to make, for instance, that changes in the social composition of the electorate would be reflected in the personnel of the House of Commons, but investigations into this subject have concluded that no such simple causal relationship existed. S. F. Woolley's pioneering work on the Parliament elected immediately after the passing of the Great Reform Act, which unfortunately has never been followed up, indicates that, if anything, the eighty-six businessmen MPs in 1833 (roughly 13 per cent of the total) represented a *decrease* in numbers compared with the unreformed Parliament. Ironically, the abolition of so many 'pocket boroughs' reduced the opportunities for wealthy businessmen, like the West Indies planters and merchants, to buy their way into the House of Commons. Nor was it invariably the case that the new urban and industrial borough constituencies, created in 1832, preferred to have businessmen as their representatives at Westminster: in fact, only 46 per cent of MPs for such seats, elected to the 1833 Parliament, were businessmen, while the majority were a mix of gentry, lawyers, military men and journalists.[20]

The salient characteristic of the British House of Commons, until the 1880s, was that it was an institution dominated by members of the aristocratic and landed class. Firmer statistics to illustrate this point are available for the Parliament of 1841–47, thanks to the work of W. O. Aydelotte, and these can be compared with analyses of the Parliaments of 1874–80 and 1886, provided by W. C. Lubenow.[21] Adopting a fairly rigorous definition of membership of the aristocratic and landed class, by confining it to Irish peers (who were eligible to sit in the Commons), the sons and grandsons of British peers, baronets and their sons and grandsons, and landed gentry and their sons and grandsons, it emerges that this group accounts for 71 per cent of MPs in 1841–47, and that the figure was still as high as 57 per cent in 1874–80, after the changes brought about by the second Reform Act had had time to show themselves. Not until the Parliament of 1886, after the third Reform Act, did the aristocratic and landed class cease to provide a majority of MPs, their numbers having fallen substantially to 37 per cent.[22] As in so many other respects, the mid-1880s seem to have marked a turning point in British parliamentary politics (see chapter 5).

Clearly, then, the long-term changes that did occur in the social composition of the House of Commons happened only very gradually, and certainly not at anything like the pace at which the electorate was being transformed. Aydelotte found that in the 1840s, 22 per cent of MPs had active and substantial business interests (in other words, they were manufacturers, merchants, bankers, chairmen of railway companies, and such like), and this figure only rose to 33 per cent in 1886, still less than that for the aristocratic and landed class. The most dynamic growth during the Victorian era involved the professions, and in particular lawyers, whose share of MPs rose from 16 per cent to 27 per cent between the 1840s and 1886, while a diverse group including academics, journalists, engineers and architects increased their share from 5 per cent to 15 per cent over the same time-span. The one social group conspicuous by its virtual absence from the House of Commons, in spite of the household suffrage provisions of the second and third Reform Acts, was the 'working class'. Two working men were returned to Parliament in 1874, and in the Parliament of 1886 there was a total of twelve so-called 'Lib-Lab' MPs, mostly representing county constituencies with a large proportion of newly-enfranchised miners. However, the Lib-Labs did not increase their numbers during the remainder of the Victorian years.

It is important to bear in mind that there is something slightly artificial about the categorisation of individuals into social groups, since in reality many MPs protrude inconveniently over the neat dividing lines drawn by historians. This is not merely a technical detail, because the fact that MPs often had overlapping economic interests is of great relevance for our understanding of why Victorian parliaments were able to function in a reasonably representative way. The House of Commons in the 1840s was, as we have seen, overwhelmingly dominated by the aristocratic and landed class, but this was partially compensated for by the fact that approximately 10 per cent of MPs from this background had, nevertheless, active and substantial business interests – typically, they would have been involved with banks, insurance companies and railway companies – and by 1886 the overlap was as high as 20 per cent. There was, in other words, no clear-cut dividing line between the interests of the traditional ruling elite and of the business community, whatever the class rhetoric of organisations like the Anti-Corn Law League may have suggested to the contrary. Similarly, there was a substantial overlap between aristocratic and landed MPs and the legal profession, because it was common practice for young men from the ruling elite to train as lawyers, not necessarily with a view to a legal career, but as a suitable preparation for their future work as legislators. On the other hand, a long-established practice survived whereby those who had pursued successful careers in business or the professions, and who entered the House of Commons, also sought to acquire social respectability, and gentility, through the possession of a landed estate and, perhaps, in due course, an hereditary title.[23]

The figures cited thus far have related to the House of Commons as a whole, and it is obviously desirable to break these down by party, so far as possible. It is no surprise to find that nearly 90 per cent of Conservative MPs in the 1840s were connected to the aristocratic and landed class,[24] but the following analysis of the Liberals shows that they were not so dissimilar from the Conservatives as might be supposed. Certainly, we must banish from our minds the simplistic notion that because the Conservative party was very largely the party of the land, the Liberals were therefore the party of business.[25]

Table 4.2 *Social composition of the Liberal Party*

Year	Aristocracy/Land (%)	Business (%)	Lawyers (%)	Miscellaneous (%)
1859	63.7	16.2	11.5	3.6
1869	51.1	24.4	13.2	5.2
1874	46.1	31.7	12.8	5.0
1886	34.2	32.0	16.2	15.0

The position after the Home Rule crisis of 1886 is less clear, in detail, but the defection of the Liberal Unionists, roughly half of whom were connected to the aristocratic and landed class,[26] undoubtedly helped to strengthen the 'middle class' element within the parliamentary Liberal Party. In the Edwardian period, it has been shown that businessmen were the largest single group amongst Liberal MPs.[27]

Rather more is known about the social composition of the

Conservative Party in the late nineteenth century, which has been researched by James Cornford. It appears from his figures, which are based on slightly different categorisations from those employed by other scholars, that in the Parliaments sitting between 1885 and 1905 roughly 40 per cent of Conservative MPs were from aristocratic and landed families, while about 31 per cent came from business backgrounds, and some 22 per cent were from the professions and public services.[28] Interestingly, Cornford shows that the relative proportions of MPs from these social groups tended to vary according to the general state of the Conservative Party. When the party did well, as in the elections of 1886, 1895 and 1900, the proportion of businessmen and professionals rose, reflecting the tendency for men from these groups to contest the more marginal seats; whereas in less auspicious times, such as 1885, 1892 and 1906, the proportion of businessmen and professionals shrank, reflecting the tendency for the aristocratic and landed interest to occupy the party's safest seats, and therefore to survive.

Two further points are worth making about the long-term shift in the social balance of the House of Commons' personnel. One is that there was a noticeable decline in the proportion of MPs who had attended public school and/or a university. Whereas in the 1841–47 Parliament, 46 per cent had been educated at a public school and 59 per cent had gone to university (overwhelmingly Oxford or Cambridge), by 1886 the respective figures were 31 per cent and 47 per cent. Secondly, the age structure of the House of Commons also underwent a significant change. In 1886, 48 per cent of MPs were over 50 years of age, and only 26 per cent were aged 40 or under, whereas in the 1840s it had been much more common for men to enter Parliament at an early age: no less than 56 per cent of MPs in 1841 were under the age of 45.[29] With the growth of 'democracy' within the British political system, it seems, the House of Commons was filled with men from a much greater diversity of backgrounds, who had less formal education than their predecessors, and were also much older.

******

To radical commentators of the early nineteenth century, such as John Wade, the author of *The Black Book,* and William Cobbett, parliamentary reform was seen as an essential precondition for a rigorous assault on the 'old corruption' which allegedly blighted the character of the British political system. They were referring to the practice, built up by politicians like Walpole in the eighteenth century, whereby governments effectively 'bought' the support of MPs through the distribution of patronage, such as pensions and sinecures (salaried appointments with no duties attached to them).[30] In fact, despite the continued criticisms levelled by Cobbett and others, the worst manifestations of 'old corruption' had been dealt with, at least as far as MPs were concerned, by a series of 'Economical Reform' measures implemented between the 1780s and the 1820s. The passing of the Great Reform Act therefore came too late to make much difference, except in the indirect sense that it helped to consolidate the new system of parliamentary politics in which ideological commitment to a party, rather than the receipt of lucrative emoluments, cemented the relationship between back-benchers and leaders. It is true, as we saw in chapter 3, that there remained important sources of patronage to which MPs needed to secure access, in order to reward their constituency supporters, and government whips exploited this situation to help ensure that MPs toed the line in the division lobby, but patronage of this sort, generally speaking, did not involve financial corruption.

Ironically, one of the great electoral reforms of the late nineteenth century, the Corrupt Practices Act of 1883, contributed, unintentionally, to the emergence of a new form of corruption which often involved MPs. The Act of 1883 set strict limits on the amount of money candidates could spend in their election contests, and it did much to put an end to the bribing of voters which had been a common feature of elections even as late as 1880, when sixteen MPs were unseated after petitions against them, alleging corrupt practices, were upheld. By helping to clean up the conduct of election campaigns in the constituencies, however, the Corrupt Practices Act encouraged greater expenditure by the political parties at the national level, at a time when, in any case, national issues and national personalities were tending to dominate the electoral battle. We know, for instance, that in 1880 the Liberal Party spent £50,000 on the general election, and that by 1910 this figure had doubled. One of the means by which the party managers raised extra sums of money was by linking donations to their war chests with the award of honours. It was demonstrated many years ago that, in 1891, two recently-elected Liberal MPs, the financier Sydney Stern and the linoleum manufacturer James Williamson, were induced to make large contributions to the Liberal Party fund in return for promises that they would receive peerages when the Liberals returned to power. There can be little doubt that the Liberal leader, Gladstone, was aware of the transaction that had taken place, and in 1895 his successor as Prime Minister, Lord Rosebery, was reluctantly obliged to fulfill the promises made to Stern and Williamson.[31] Such practices were not confined to the Liberal side, though, for we now know that the Liberal Unionists used their alliance with Salisbury's Conservative government in order to obtain honours for certain supporters, who were required to make donations to the fund being raised to fight the 1892 general election. In this case, baronetcies were given to a Birmingham businessman who was retiring from the House of Commons, a former MP, and a prominent Birmingham newspaper proprietor. The Conservatives took a 'cut' of the monies paid.[32] These episodes in the early 1890s marked the beginning of a form of corrupt practice which was to get seriously out of hand during the Lloyd George era, in the 1910s and 1920s, when the sale of honours became a national scandal.[33]

If anything can be said in extenuation for the sale of honours, it would have to be that it provided an opportunity for successful businessmen, and others, to be absorbed into the political 'Establishment'. By no means all of the men who resorted to this means of obtaining the social recognition they desired were MPs, of course, but there is no doubt that for many from the middle classes, who did enter the House of Commons, the purchase of an hereditary title enabled them to 'cap' their social ascent. The main difference between the 1890s and earlier decades was that it was no longer necessary for such men to first acquire a landed estate, and the social respectability pertaining to it, in order to qualify themselves for an honour. Looked at from a positive point of view, what the sale of honours demonstrates is the remarkable capacity for the British parliamentary system to integrate old and new elements.

Notes

1 C. Cook and B. Keith, *British Historical Facts, 1830–1900* (London, 1975), p. 115.

2 See Norman Gash, *Politics in the Age of Peel*, 2nd edn., (Brighton, 1977).

3 Derek Beales, 'The Electorate before and after 1832: the Right to Vote, and the Opportunity', *Parliamentary History*, XI (1992), pp. 139–50. This is a review of Frank O'Gorman's *Voters, Patrons and Parties: The Unreformed Electoral System of Hanoverian England, 1734–1832* (Oxford, 1989), which seeks to play down the significance of the changes made in 1832.

4 James Cornford, 'The Transformation of Conservatism in the Late Nineteenth Century', *Victorian Studies*, VI (1963), pp. 35–66.

5 Nancy LoPatin, 'Political Unions and the Great Reform Act', *Parliamentary History*, X (1991), pp. 105–23.

6 Roland Quinault, 'The French Revolution of 1830 and Parliamentary Reform', *History*, LXXIX (1994), pp. 377–93.

7 Wellington's 'Protestant' stance on this issue had alienated some Liberal Tories in 1828, but his subsequent surrender to the Catholics' demands, in 1829, alienated many 'ultra-Tories'. G. I. T. Machin, *The Catholic Question in English Politics, 1820–30* (Oxford, 1964).

8 J. Milton Smith, 'Earl Grey's Cabinet and the Objects of Parliamentary Reform', *Historical Journal*, XV (1972), pp. 55–74; Michael Brock, *The Great Reform Act* (London, 1973).

9 Jonathan Parry, *The Rise and Fall of Liberal Government in Victorian Britain* (Yale, 1993), pp. 84, 86.

10 Roland Quinault, '1848 and Parliamentary Reform', *Historical Journal*, XXXI (1988), pp. 831–51.

11 Brand to Sir George Grey, 9 December 1859, Brand MSS (HLRO), vol. I; Brand to Russell (copy), 30 May 1860, Broadlands MSS (Southampton University Library), GC/BR/6.

12 H. C. G. Matthew, *Gladstone, 1809–74* (Oxford, 1986), pp. 109–28. More generally, see F. B. Smith, *The Making of the Second Reform Bill* (Cambridge, 1966).

13 J. M. Winter, *Robert Lowe* (Toronto, 1976), pp. 195–226.

14 Maurice Cowling, 'Disraeli, Derby and Fusion, October 1865 to July 1866', *Historical Journal*, VIII (1965), pp. 31–71.

15 Robert Stewart, *The Foundation of the Conservative Party, 1830–1867* (London, 1978), pp. 352–66, usefully relates the 1859 and 1867 bills.

16 There is some dispute as to whether or not Salisbury desired a settlement all along, and as to the role of the Queen in forcing Salisbury to settle. See the debate between Corinne C. Weston, 'Disunity on the Opposition Front Bench, 1884', and John D. Fair, 'The Carnarvon Diaries and Royal Mediation in 1884', *English Historical Review*, CV1 (1991), pp. 80–116.

17   Mary E. J. Chadwick, 'The Role of Redistribution in the Making of the Third Reform Act', *Historical Journal*, XIX (1976), pp. 665–83.

18   Neal Blewett, 'The Franchise in the United Kingdom, 1885–1918', *Past and Present*, XXXII (1965), pp. 27–56.

19   Duncan Tanner, 'The Parliamentary Electoral System, the "Fourth" Reform Act and the Rise of Labour in England and Wales', *Bulletin of the Institute of Historical Research*, LVI (1983), pp. 205–19.

20   S. F. Woolley, 'The Personnel of the Parliament of 1833', *English Historical Review*, LIII (1938), pp. 240–62. There is also J. A. Thomas, *The House of Commons 1832–1901: A Study of its Economic and Functional Character* (Cardiff, 1939), but this makes no attempt to distinguish between MPs' major and minor economic interests.

21   W. O. Aydelotte, 'The House of Commons in the 1840s', *History*, XXXIX (1954), pp. 249–62; W. C. Lubenow, *Parliamentary Politics and the Home Rule Crisis: The British House of Commons in 1886* (Oxford, 1988), pp. 54–66, 168–74. Lubenow draws upon an unpublished dissertation by Dr J. C. Hamilton for the 1874–80 Parliament.

22   It might be noted that if those MPs with aristocratic and landed connections through the maternal line, or through marriage, are also included, the figures would be 80 per cent, 67 per cent and 45 per cent, respectively.

23   R. Pumphrey, 'The Introduction of Industrialists into the British Peerage: A Study in Adaptation of a Social Institution', *American Historical Review*, LXV (1959), pp. 1–16.

24   W. O. Aydelotte, 'The Country Gentlemen and the Repeal of the Corn Laws', *English Historical Review*, LXXXII (1967), p. 54.

25   T. A. Jenkins, *The Liberal Ascendancy, 1830–1886* (London, 1994), pp. 105, 127, 146, 198. It was not possible to find information about every MP.

26   *Ibid.*, p. 212.

27   G. R. Searle, 'The Edwardian Liberal Party and Business', *English Historical Review*, XCVIII (1983), pp. 28–60.

28   James Cornford, 'The Parliamentary Foundations of the Hotel Cecil', in Robert Robson (ed.), *Ideas and Institutions of Victorian Britain* (London, 1967), especially pp. 277, 310.

29   Aydelotte, 'House of Commons in 1840s', pp. 253–4; Lubenow, *British House of Commons in 1886*, pp. 53–4.

30   W. D. Rubinstein, 'The End of "Old Corruption" in Britain,

1780–1860', *Past and Present*, CI (1983), pp. 55–86. This was part of a wider nexus of patronage embracing the Church, the law courts and the armed forces.

31   H. J. Hanham, 'The Sale of Honours in Late Victorian England', *Victorian Studies*, III (1960), pp. 277–89.

32   T. A. Jenkins, 'The Funding of the Liberal Unionist Party and the Honours System', *English Historical Review*, CV (1990), pp. 920–38.

33   G. R. Searle, *Corruption in British Politics, 1895–1930* (Oxford, 1987).

5

The triumph of partisan politics, 1867–1900

Historians have customarily taken the view that the passing of the second Reform Act, in 1867, was *the* decisive event in shaping the course of late-Victorian politics. The Conservatives, abandoning their old tactic of seeking to fuse with moderate elements from the Liberal Party, had instead gambled on the benefits of being seen to have settled the Reform question, by passing a far-reaching measure enfranchising large numbers of working men in the boroughs. This display of opportunism alarmed many contemporary politicians, including moderate Liberals, who feared that the Conservatives had injected a dangerously unstable element into the Constitution which might prove inimical to the conduct of 'good government' (see Doc. 10). There are indeed some indications that the new voters were more partisan in their political attitudes: for instance, in two-member constituencies the electors had two votes to cast, and it seems that in the 1868 general election the practive of 'splitting' the votes between candidates of different parties was much less common than had previously been the case.[1] One consequence of the newly-enlarged electorate, which has always been emphasised by scholars, was the stimulus given to the development of party organisation in the constituencies, and to the creation of national forums in which these organisations could make their voice heard. Thus the National Union of Conservative and Constitutional Associations (National Union) was founded in 1867, and the National Liberal Federation (NLF) followed in 1877. At the same time, the need for politicians to address a vastly increased audience encouraged a more confrontational, even personalised, style of politics,

111

which was exemplified by the titanic duel between Gladstone and Disraeli culminating in the dramatic Midlothian campaigns of 1879–80. Inevitably, this changed environment produced a new breed of politician, such as the radical, Joseph Chamberlain, whose power base rested largely on his ability to manipulate the party machine, and on his hold over popular audiences.

It is certainly not the object of this chapter to assert that the above view of the character of late-Victorian politics is entirely wrong, but it can be suggested that '1867' was not quite the watershed that it is supposed to be, and that the changes attributed to the Reform Act of that year occurred much more gradually. Above all, it is hoped to demonstrate that many of the features of parliamentary politics discussed in chapter 2 survived long into the more 'democratic' world of the post-1867 era.

The growth of extra-parliamentary party organisation provides a good illustration of the way that the pace and extent of change can easily be exaggerated. That important developments were taking place is not in question, but the Conservative National Union, for example, did not consist of local associations organised on anything like a democratic basis. Control was usually in the hands of a middle-class elite of local businessmen and professional people. Furthermore, local Conservative Associations were essentially an urban phenomenon, for it was in the large boroughs that the party most needed to build up its support, whereas in its traditional county strongholds electoral politics continued to operate on the familiar basis of landlord influence. Some Liberal MPs, it should be remembered, also represented county constituencies, and many more sat for small boroughs which were not dissimilar in character. The NLF, which was not established until ten years after the second Reform Act, did at least give the appearance of being organised on the democratic principle: anyone who paid the subscription was eligible to join a local association, and they could play a part in the election of the local executive, which in turn sent delegates to the annual conference of the NLF. In practice, however, it was possible for a small minority of middle-class activists, with money and therefore time on their hands, to pull the strings of these Liberal organisations. More importantly, the title *National* Liberal Federation is seriously misleading, because the NLF in its early years was nothing like a body representative of the whole country. Its headquarters, significantly, were in Birmingham, and regional organisations based in Scotland,

Wales, London and the Home Counties, and Manchester, would have nothing to do with it. The NLF, for all its claims to articulate the views of the newly-enfranchised people, in reality served as the mouthpiece of a sectional group within the Liberal Party, the Birmingham radicals, dominated by Joseph Chamberlain. For all these reasons, therefore, it would be a mistake to envisage the political system shortly after the second Reform Act as one that was dominated by democratically-elected local caucuses affiliated to powerful national federations; although it is true, as we shall see, that further developments in this direction were in evidence from the mid-1880s onwards.[2]

W. E. Gladstone's career, during the 1860s and early 1870s, is highly instructive as to the realities of the political system. While Chancellor of the Exchequer in Palmerston's second ministry, Gladstone emerged as the leading exponent of an extra-parliamentary style of political leadership by addressing large audiences in provincial towns such as Newcastle and Manchester. In this way, he was able to cultivate the support of a wide variety of social groups, including businessmen, Nonconformists, radical reformers and working men, and he exploited his popularity with the public in order to enhance his authority at Westminster and mark himself out as a future leader of the Liberal Party. So diverse was his appeal that he even managed to reintegrate the Irish Brigade into the main body of Liberals, by declaring his support for Church disestablishment in Ireland. This issue indeed provided a unifying cause for all Liberals, under Gladstone's leadership, during the general election of 1868, the first under the system of borough household suffrage, and the result was a spectacular triumph for the party, which gained a majority of about 110.[3]

Nevertheless, it remained the case that skilful management of the House of Commons was crucial to the success of any premiership, and the fate of Gladstone's first ministry (1868–74) shows that it was still possible for a government possessing a large majority on paper to run into serious difficulties. There were obviously many reasons for the collapse in the morale and cohesion of the Liberals in the House of Commons during the early 1870s, but Gladstone's personal deficiencies as a parliamentary leader undoubtedly contributed to the problem. Liberal unity had held up well while the government was passing its Irish Church and Land bills, in 1869–70, but there were already signs in 1870 that a loss of political momentum was being suffered

113

due to the unpopularity of the Education bill, which offended many radicals and Nonconformists by failing to challenge the Church of England's dominant role within the education system. Other measures, such as the Licensing bills of 1871 and 1872, also alienated powerful interest groups in the country. In these more adverse circumstances, the government's ambitious legislative programme ran into major obstacles at Westminster. It was easy, once the government's standing with public opinion no longer seemed secure, for Conservative MPs to take advantage of the antiquated procedures of the House of Commons in order to obstruct measures like the Army Regulation bill and Ballot bill, in 1871. There was, after all, no limit to the number of times MPs could move for the adjournment of a debate, and this device was sometimes used several times in one evening to ensure that time was wasted in debating and dividing on the proposed adjournments. With sittings of the House sometimes lasting well into the early hours of the morning, exhaustion and demoralisation spread through the Liberal ranks, and became a cause of great concern to the government's chief whip (see Doc. 23).

To some extent, it is fair to say that the difficulties encountered by Gladstone's ministry reflected badly both upon Conservative MPs, and on the capacity of Parliament, under its existing rules, to act as an instrument of major legislative change. (In 1871, of 111 public bills introduced, 28 had to be abandoned, and in 1873 24 bills out of 104 were similarly lost.) The situation was aggravated, though, by the fact that Gladstone proved temperamentally unsuited to the task of steering a party out of deep political waters, and, most worryingly of all, that he found it increasingly difficult to keep his temper with the House of Commons. The front-bench Conservative, Gathorne Hardy, was the victim of one Gladstonian eruption, in February 1872, when he made a speech criticising the Prime Minister which provoked 'such an explosion of passion & temper from Gladstone as even he has seldom exhibited. Constant storms followed. His abuse of me amused me a good deal more than hurt me. He could scarcely get it out for rage. What a leader of the House'. Concerns were meantime being expressed on the Liberal side about the damage Gladstone was doing to his authority. The nadir of his fortunes was reached in March 1873, when the government's Irish University bill, pressed on in spite of its unpopularity with Irish

Roman Catholics and some British radicals, was defeated by three votes. So humiliating was this reverse that Gladstone and his colleagues tendered their resignations, although in the event Disraeli's unwillingness to form an alternative government meant that they were obliged to return to office.[4]

If it is now clear that, for all the undoubted changes in British political life influenced by the second Reform Act, the parliamentary arena continued to be of critical importance, and was at least partially autonomous in the way it operated, it is instructive to look again at the evidence of MPs' voting behaviour. In chapter 2, we saw that the majority of parliamentary divisions on government questions (i.e. 'whip' divisions), between the 1830s and the 1860s, did not involve a conflict between government and opposition, and that in many cases the two front benches actually co-operated with one another. Hugh Berrington's analysis shows that this pattern of voting survived to a very large extent even in the 1870s and early 1880s. In the table below, which is a continuation of Table 2.1, it will be remembered that 'True two-party votes' were those in which at least 90 per cent of party members on both sides voted with their leaders, 'Cross-bench votes' were those in which moderate MPs from one party voted with the other party against the wishes of their own leaders, and 'Extremist votes' were those where the majority of members of both parties voted together against a group such as the radicals.[5]

Table 5.1   *Voting behaviour in the House of Commons*

Year	Number of whip divisions	True Two-party votes (%)	Cross-bench votes (%)	Extremist votes (%)
1836	88	34	33	33
1850	221	18	42	41
1860	173	5	46	50
1871	209	38	38	24
1881	170	49	16	35
1883	194	35	20	45

As the post-1867 figures suggest, there was some increase in political partisanship, in the sense that government and opposition leaders were more likely than before to be in direct conflict in the division lobbies, but the change was hardly dramatic, and even in the session of 1881 – a relatively tempestuous one, in which the Liberal ministry was pushing through the second Irish Land bill – it did not quite reach one half of 'whip' votes. It is of particular interest that by the early 1880s 'extremist dissidence' was on the increase again, reflecting the difficulties experienced by Gladstone's second ministry (1880–85) in producing a bold programme of reforming legislation likely to maintain the enthusiasm of its more radical back-benchers. Consequently, we find that in the 1883 session of Parliament there was considerable cooperation between the two front benches, designed to resist radical attempts to reduce government expenditure and to amend government measures such as the Agricultural Holdings bill and the Corrupt Practices bill.[6]

Another important feature of pre-1867 parliamentary politics which survived for many years after the second Reform Act, was the way that opposition leaders still tended to look towards the disintegration of the governing party, rather than to the next general election, as the most likely path back to office. This may seem surprising, as the general elections of 1868, 1874 and 1880, which produced large majorities first for the Liberals, then the Conservatives, then the Liberals again, have given rise to the popular notion that this was the 'classic age of the two-party system'. But it was only afterwards, when looking back at this period of sharp electoral fluctuations, that politicians and journalists began to talk of a natural 'swing of the pendulum', meaning that the party that had lost an election could expect to benefit from the changing tide of public opinion next time around. If we look at the reality of the situation as it was perceived by Disraeli, after the Conservative defeat in 1868, it was clear to him that a policy of 'utmost reserve and quietness' was the order of the day, rather than trying to fling the Conservative Party against the brickwall of a Liberal majority of 110, and that he must look to an eventual falling out between the government and its more radical followers.[7] One of Disraeli's colleagues recorded in his diary, in May 1870, a conversation in which Disraeli stated that 'he looks forward to Gladstone becoming useless to the Radicals & a disruption. Gives two years or more'. Indeed, it was during the 1870 session of Parliament that Disraeli was able to make a start in the pursuit of his objective, when he took care to *support* Gladstone's ministry in the division lobby on its controversial

116

Education bill, which had infuriated many Liberals: by helping to save the bill from defeat, of course, Disraeli was also driving in the wedge between the government and its own back-bench dissidents – precisely the tactic that his old leader, Derby, had sought to utilise in the 1850s and 1860s. (It should be noted that many of the instances of Conservative obstructionism, notably when the 'Tory Colonels' went on the rampage against the Army Regulation bill, were the work of uncontrollable back-benchers, not of the party leaders.) When Gladstone's ministry resigned in March 1873, after the defeat of its Irish University bill, Disraeli significantly rejected the opportunity to form yet another minority Conservative government, and was determined to force the Liberals to remain in office until the process of disintegration was complete, for he was still not certain that an early general election would produce a Conservative majority. This decision was dramatically vindicated when Gladstone's ministry encountered further parliamentary difficulties, including the scandals surrounding the use of Post Office revenues and the awarding of a mail contract in Africa, which necessitated the removal or reshuffling of a number of ministers. The government limped on until January 1874, when Gladstone took a desperate gamble on a sudden dissolution of Parliament, which resulted in an electoral disaster for the Liberal Party going far beyond what contemporary observers had anticipated.

So shocked were the Liberals by their heavy defeat – it was the first time since 1841 that the Conservatives had secured an overall majority in the House of Commons – that few expected that it would be possible to reverse the party positions after just one general election. Consequently the Liberal leaders were also inclined to look to the eventual disintegration of the Conservatives as their best hope of political salvation, though this was expected to be a long-term process. During the crisis over the Eastern Question, therefore, when war between Britain and Russia seemed possible, the opposition front bench generally refrained from voting against the government, partly from fear of appearing 'unpatriotic' at a time of national emergency, but also in the hope of strengthening the position of the 'doves' against the 'hawks' within the Cabinet. In December 1877, Lord Granville, the leader of the Liberal peers, expressed the opinion that 'the pear is certainly not yet ripe for us . . . it will take a long course of discredit really to break up the Conservative party'. There were some promising signs in this direction, early in 1878, when two Cabinet ministers, Lords Carnarvon and Derby, resigned because of their alarm at Disraeli's belligerent stance towards Russia, and it was hoped that these peers would gravitate towards the Liberal side (only Derby did so, in the event). The most likely future catalyst for a Conservative schism, however, was deemed to be the choice of a successor to Disraeli (created Earl of Beaconsfield in 1876), who was in his seventies and often in poor health, and the prospect of the abrasive and reputedly reactionary Marquis of Salisbury as the next Conservative leader seemed likely to be especially productive in terms of the alienation of moderate Conservatives, who might then be attracted over to the Liberal side.[8]

An unexpectedly decisive general election result in April 1880, this time in the Liberals' favour, once again transformed the situation, but it is interesting to note that in the immediate aftermath of the Conservative defeat, Sir Stafford Northcote, now leader of the opposition in the House of Commons, was calculating on the possible disruption of the Liberal majority. As he confided to his diary, 'I think it is likely enough that a conservative cave may be formed on the Liberal side ... and that if we manage our opposition discreetly, we may often join hands with them, and perhaps ultimately bring some of them to take part in a Conservative Cabinet'.[9] Northcote's belief that the Conservatives should adopt a strategy of moderation, in order to attract Liberals alarmed by the radical tendencies of Gladstone's new government, was to be rudely challenged by the antics of the 'Fourth Party' (as we shall soon see), but it is worth bearing in mind that the course preferred by Northcote was in line with the one frequently adopted by previous opposition leaders. If nothing more, Northcote was a conventional parliamentarian pursuing a conventional parliamentary strategy.

If opposition practices, at least until the early 1880s, conformed to an earlier pattern, this is similarly true of the organisational structure of parties when in opposition. Meetings of the opposition leadership – the term 'shadow Cabinet' did not come into use until the Edwardian period – in order to settle party tactics do seem to have taken place more frequently than was generally the case before 1867, and it was more common for peers and

MPs to consult together, but there were still no established rules determining when meetings should be called and who was eligible to attend. A great deal of discretion in these matters was still retained by the party leader, and in the 1868–74 and 1874–80 Parliaments, the overall impression from the surviving evidence is that those meetings that were held usually involved no more than about half a dozen prominent party members.[10] In the case of the Conservative opposition of 1868–74, *ad hoc* groups of leading party figures, interested in a particular area of policy, are known to have met occasionally. Meetings between the party leader and the parliamentary rank and file also continued, as in the past, to be exceptional events, usually prompted by some emergency, rather than a routine method of binding together leaders and followers. The Conservatives (and this point applies when they were in government as well as in opposition) do not appear to have held party meetings on average more than once or twice in any parliamentary session. Liberal meetings were rarer still: apart from the gathering of MPs at the Reform Club, in February 1875, which endorsed Hartington as their new Commons leader, there is no evidence of any meetings at all taking place while the party was in opposition between 1874 and 1880.

******

Two case-studies will enable us to examine in more detail the tensions that were often created because of differing approaches to the way political life ought to be conducted in the environment created by the second Reform Act. These studies involve the Liberal opposition in the years from 1875, when Gladstone resigned as leader, until 1880, and the subsequent period of Conservative opposition lasting until 1885. Certain important features were common to both oppositions: each had a dual leadership – Granville in the Lords and Hartington in the Commons, for the Liberals, and (after Beaconsfield's death in 1881), Salisbury in the Lords and Northcote in the Commons for the Conservatives – and in each case a shift took place in the balance of power between the dual leaders, to the detriment of Granville and Northcote. Furthermore, both House of Commons leaders had to contend with problems arising from the conduct of other members of their respective parties. Hartington might have expected the more radically inclined of his back-benchers to cause him trouble from time to time, but he had the added difficulty of dealing with the former leader, Gladstone, who sometimes took an independent line. Northcote's worries were somewhat different, for they were caused by a back-bench ginger group, the 'Fourth Party', who seemed determined to undermine his authority as leader. To a qualified extent, it is fair to regard these case-studies as representing the contrast between 'old' and 'new' styles of political action.

Gladstone had resigned the Liberal leadership of his own accord, in January 1875, because he felt disillusioned with the factious behaviour displayed by the party during his first administration. On the other hand, the succession of Hartington, the heir of the Duke of Devonshire and thus a representative of the 'Whig' tradition of aristocratic Liberalism, was seen by many as indicative of the Liberals' need for a less erratic and tempestuous style of leadership than that provided by Gladstone.[11] Hartington's position was inevitably complicated, however, by the fact that the former leader, twenty-four years Hartington's senior, chose to remain in the House of Commons and considered himself to be at liberty to pursue a separate course when he differed from the new leader. (There are certain interesting parallels here, of course, with the problems Mr Major faced with Mrs Thatcher, in 1990–92.) The revival of the Eastern Question in 1876, prompted by Turkey's savage suppression of an uprising by her Christian subjects in Bulgaria, served to raise the political temperature in Britain to a level guaranteed to bring out the differences in outlook between the passionately committed Gladstone and the phlegmatically detached Hartington.[12] Gladstone's response to the news of the Bulgarian atrocities was to publish a pamphlet on the subject, which became a best-seller when it appeared in September, and in December he addressed a national conference on the Eastern Question held at St James's Hall, Piccadilly. For the next eighteen months, Gladstone made speeches, both in and out of Parliament, denouncing the barbarous Turks, but also condemning the complicity of Beaconsfield's government, which had refused to join in international efforts to coerce Turkey into granting reforms in her subject provinces. Hartington, meantime, remained wary of launching any party attack on the government, sharing as he did Beaconsfield's concern about possible Russian territorial expansion in the guise of aid for the oppressed peoples of the Balkans, and judging – perhaps rightly – that Russophobia was the dominant sentiment within British public opinion. The consequent divisions in the Liberal ranks reached crisis point during the 1878 session of Parliament, when Gladstone sided with radicals like John Bright and Sir Wilfrid Lawson in opposing military preparations for a possible war with Russia, while the opposition front bench walked out of the House.

We must be careful, though, not to exaggerate the contrast between Hartington and Gladstone's political styles. In fact, Gladstone's involvement in the 'Bulgarian agitation' was marked throughout by ambiguity towards the idea of extra-parliamentary action.[13] At heart he was a sincere parliamentarian, anxious to see the House of Commons fulfill its role as *the* arena for national political debate: the publication of the pamphlet, and the speech at the St James's Hall conference, could be justified on the grounds that the Bulgarian atrocities had come to public prominence during the autumn and winter of 1876, when Parliament was not in session. Furthermore, it is interesting to note that he always maintained a polite distance between himself and the Eastern Question Association, the campaigning organisation which had grown out of the conference in December 1876. But the unavoidable reality of the parliamentary situation – that the Liberals were in a minority, and that in any case many disapproved of Gladstone's conduct – meant that he was driven increasingly to recognise the need to look beyond Westminster. For instance, his decision to accept an invitation to address the inaugural conference of Chamberlain's National Liberal Federation, in Birmingham in May 1877, followed closely on the embarrassing failure of a series of resolutions on the Eastern Question which he had put forward in the House of Commons. The decisive moment for Gladstone, in his reluctant evolution into an extra-parliamentary campaigner, came when he accepted the Liberal candidature for the Conservative-held seat of Midlothian, and used the opportunity this provided to launch two spectacular series of public speeches, in 1879–80, in which he furiously condemned what he considered to be an evil system of government in Britain – 'Beaconsfieldism'.

As for Hartington, while it is true that he could never hope to compete with Gladstone in whipping up popular fervour through speeches, it would be wrong to suppose that he was merely the diametric opposite of Gladstone, in other words, an old-fashioned parliamentarian wedded to outmoded techniques of political leadership. We have already noted that Hartington was a much younger man than Gladstone, and his career provides a good illustration of the way that all serious politicians were coming to terms with the requirements of a more democratic, participatory system. It is noteworthy that in the winter of 1876 Hartington did not object at all to the Liberals holding public meetings to criticise the government, but he was sceptical about the efficacy of the proposed national conference in London, believing that it was 'almost sure to get principally into the hands of men of extreme opinions, who would make speeches under no sense of responsibility whatever'.[14] More importantly still, Hartington himself became a regular performer on the public 'stump', so much so that on one occasion he jokingly remarked that he would probably 'have to leave the Country' in order to escape the numerous invitations to speak.[15] During the 1880 general election campaign, it was calculated that Hartington was the most active public speaker of all, making twenty-four major orations compared with Gladstone's fifteen. It was precisely because Hartington had succeeded in enhancing his public reputation, since assuming the Liberal leadership, that after the general election Queen Victoria, who detested Gladstone because of his attacks on her beloved Beaconsfield, invited Hartington to form a government. In the event, Hartington judged that it would be prudent for him to make way for Gladstone, at least temporarily, since it was clear that Gladstone would not serve in a Hartington administration, and that he might well become a dangerous critic if left on the back-benches.[16] Nevertheless, the crucial point for our purposes is that the late 1870s witnessed important developments in terms of the technique of political opposition, with the Liberals (and not only Gladstone, supreme exponent of popular oratory though he was) taking the issues of the day out of Parliament and to the country directly.

Our second case-study, relating to the Conservative opposition in the early 1880s, provides a more striking contrast between the 'old' and 'new' styles of political action. The 1880 session of Parliament was much preoccupied with the controversy surrounding the attempts by the atheistic Liberal MP for Northampton,

Charles Bradlaugh, to take his seat in the House of Commons.
A small group of back-bench Conservatives, jocularly known as
the 'Fourth Party', emerged at the forefront of the opposition
to Bradlaugh: essentially, there were just three members of this
'party', the young aristocrat, Lord Randolph Churchill, and two
older malcontents, John Eldon Gorst and Henry Drummond
Wolff (Arthur Balfour, who is sometimes included, was never
more than casually associated with them). [17] In seizing upon
the Bradlaugh affair, the Fourth Party was able to articulate the
sense of outrage felt by many Conservatives at the prospect of
an avowed atheist being allowed to sit in the House of Commons, and it also provided a useful weapon with which to attack
Gladstone's government and the Liberal Party, which, it could
be implied, were full of closet sympathisers with the atheist. At
the same time, the impact of the Fourth Party's campaign was
indicative of a strong current of feeling against the Conservative
leadership, in a party that was still suffering from the shock of
the 1880 general election defeat. On 24 May 1880, 191 Conservative MPs, over two-thirds of the entire party, voted for Wolff's
motion to refuse to allow Bradlaugh to take the parliamentary
oath, and as a result Northcote, the official leader in the Commons
since Disraeli's elevation to the peerage in 1876, was obliged to
join in the subsequent efforts to block Bradlaugh's admission.
This episode appeared to be symptomatic of the effete leadership
offered by Northcote and his front-bench colleagues – they were
often referred to collectively and contemptuously, by the Fourth
Party, as 'the old gang' or 'the goats' – which was, as we saw
earlier, aimed at trying to conciliate and win over nervous moderate Liberals. Apart from the Bradlaugh affair, which was to be
a recurring focus for heated argument for several years to come,
Churchill and his friends also launched vigorous assaults on the
Gladstone ministry over such issues as the Irish Land bill of
1881. Their style was reminiscent of that of a group of impish
schoolboys, taking delight in shocking their elders, and they were
particularly effective in baiting Gladstone, whose earnestness and
loquacity made him a perfect target. Churchill himself acquired
some expertese in the details of parliamentary procedure, and
was often able to use this to good effect in wasting time during
debates. Indeed, their critics alleged that the Fourth Party was as
guilty as Parnell and the Irish Home Rulers (the two groups

often co-operated) in obstructing the progress of government business in the House of Commons.

Simultaneously with his parliamentary antics, Churchill made a big impact with his provincial speaking tours, developing a style of popular oratory characterised by exuberance, hyperbole, flights of fancy, and often sheer rudeness towards opponents. To many observers, it seemed that he was injecting a regrettable tone of vulgarity into the public discussion of political affairs. Nevertheless, he succeeded in identifying himself, in the public mind, with the concept of 'Tory Democracy', however nebulous this may have been in terms of concrete policies. Churchill's cultivation of links with the press, notably the *Morning Post* and the weekly society journal, *Vanity Fair*, likewise showed him to be an accomplished practitioner of the arts of self-advertisement, an area in which the competent, intelligent, but uninspiring and fatally decent Northcote, over thirty years Churchill's senior, had little hope of being able to compete. For a short period, in 1883–84, Churchill also interested himself in the affairs of the Conservative National Union, exploiting the discontent of many provincial activists by making himself the focus for a campaign to reform the management of the party.

Exactly what Churchill's original intentions towards Northcote may have been are not entirely certain, but by 1883 (he missed most of the 1882 session through illness) it was evident that his object was to destroy Northcote's leadership and establish Lord Salisbury's overall authority over the Conservative Party (see Doc. 26). In doing so, of course, Churchill's aim was to set himself up as Salisbury's indispensable lieutenant in the House of Commons. After all, Salisbury's distaste for Churchill's methods may have been genuine enough, but he was also well aware of the advantages to himself of Northcote's plight. During the spring of 1883 Churchill launched a series of direct personal attacks on Northcote, in letters to *The Times*, and in a famous article in the May edition of the *Fortnightly Review*, entitled 'Elijah's Mantle'. Significantly, however, as the reception given to these attacks on Northcote shows, Churchill still ran the risk of offending the more conventionally-minded Conservative back-benchers, who felt that he was going too far, and who in fact publicly rallied to the support of their official leader.[18] The cumulative effect of Churchill's activities, nevertheless, was to undermine Northcote's position to such an extent that when the Conservatives were asked to form a government, in June 1885, the Queen entrusted the task to Salisbury. At this point, Churchill refused to serve in the new government if Northcote remained in the House of Commons, and the result was that the unfortunate 'goat' had to be consoled with a peerage while, for the sake of appearance, Sir Michael Hicks Beach, a recent ally of Churchill's, assumed the leadership of the House of Commons. Churchill then agreed to take office as Secretary of State for India. A little over a year later, his personal triumph appeared to be complete when, on the formation of Salisbury's second ministry (after the Home Rule crisis), Churchill was appointed Chancellor of the Exchequer and Leader of the House of Commons, at the age of only 37. The lesson for all ambitious politicians seemed to be that the methods associated with Churchill provided the key to personal advancement, but the limits to his position were brutally exposed in December 1886, when he overreached himself against Salisbury by threatening to resign over policy differences (his bluff was called), with the result that he was driven into the political wilderness. It was to be Salisbury, the last peer-Prime Minister, whose apparent remoteness and unworldliness disguised the fact that he was an acute and cynical political operator, who became the dominant figure in late-Victorian Conservatism, remaining at the top until his retirement in 1902.[19]

In addition to these case-studies of the Liberal and Conservative oppositions, the gradual change in the conduct of politics is most vividly demonstrated by the radical campaign initiated by Joseph Chamberlain, in 1885. Chamberlain had been a minister in Gladstone's second government, which succeeded in passing the third Reform Act (implementing household suffrage in the counties) and securing a sweeping redistribution of seats, before it resigned in June 1885 after a defeat on the budget. This released Chamberlain to campaign for the radical policies which he believed would secure the allegiance of the new electorate to the Liberal Party. *The Radical Programme*, a collection of articles discussing a wide range of ideas, was published, and from this Chamberlain concentrated on three issues, free education, graduated taxation, and allotments for rural labourers, which became known as the 'Unauthorised Programme' (because it was not the official policy of the Liberal Party). During the long autumn election campaign, lasting from September to early December, Chamberlain worked vigorously to promote his programme through public speeches, confident that he could force all Liberal candidates to adopt his policies in order to secure the new voters. But Chamberlain's campaign ran into all sorts of difficulties, partly because many Nonconformists were unhappy that he did not take a stronger line against the Church of England, and also because many radicals (as well as mainstream Liberals, including Gladstone), disliked the 'socialistic' tendencies inherent in his policies. At the end of the day, therefore, he was unable to impose his programme upon the Liberal Party.[20] The 'Unauthorised Programme' is nevertheless of considerable historical interest, for it was the first attempt to appeal to the electorate with a specific set of policies, rather than merely relying on general declarations of principle, as in the past, and as such it anticipated the politics of the twentieth century, in which party programmes have become the accepted norm. Furthermore, Chamberlain's campaign in 1885 is significant for the response it provoked from other Liberals, not only Gladstone (who appeared again at Midlothian), but also Hartington and other moderates like G. J. Goschen, all of whom were compelled to counter Chamberlain's speeches with speeches of their own, and to be more specific in their own policy prescriptions (though they did not go so far as to issue 'programmes'). In order to survive, Chamberlain's Liberal rivals had to go a long way towards adopting his political methods (see Doc. 11).

******

In December 1868 the Earl of Kimberley, who had just been appointed to Gladstone's first administration, recorded in his journal a conversation with a leading Conservative, Lord Stanley (soon to succeed his father as the 15th Earl of Derby), in which the latter had spoken about his political position. Kimberley gained the impression that Stanley's 'dream is to be at the head of a coalition between the Whigs & the moderate Conservatives', but his own view of this was very different:

> Such a coalition is often talked about. I doubt whether it will ever take place. I doubt still more whether if it did, it would be beneficial to the Country. The Radicals would then form a party by themselves. The Whigs would insensibly be merged with the

moderate Conservatives in the Tory party. The result would be greater violence in party warfare, and the loss of that tacit understanding between the leaders on both sides which has much more to do with the smooth working of our complex political system than superficial observers, who only see the outside of public affairs, imagine.[21]

Certainly, the changes associated with the extended franchise of 1867 (and perpetuated by the further instalment of reform in 1884), such as the growth of extra-parliamentary organisation, and the use of new techniques by ambitious politicians of the Churchill and Chamberlain stamp seeking to appeal to the electorate, injected a greater degree of 'violence' into 'party warfare' than had hitherto been the case. But the sort of cross-party collaboration desired by Kimberley was, in fact, substantially maintained into the 1880s, as we saw earlier in relation to the evidence of MPs' voting behaviour. This leads us to the suggestion that the realignment of parties, following the Irish Home Rule crisis of 1886, was at least as important as the earlier franchise reforms in polarising the British political system.

The 'Irish Question' had entered a new phase during the 1870s, with the formation of an independent Home Rule Party in the House of Commons, led by Isaac Butt, whose existence reflected Irish disillusionment with the policies of Gladstone's first ministry. By the end of that decade, the Home Rule Party was being increasingly radicalised as it came under the control of Charles Stewart Parnell. Parnell pursued a two-pronged approach to the campaign for Home Rule, combining a policy of deliberate obstructionism at Westminster with support for the Land League in Ireland, which was exploiting the discontent caused by the agricultural depression of the late 1870s. Both Parnellite strategies, challenging firstly the supremacy of Parliament, and secondly the rights of landlords, were well designed to provoke the antagonism of the British political establishment, and as early as 1880 the Conservatives tried, without much success, to make an election issue out of the Liberals' alleged sympathy with the Home Rulers. Gladstone's second ministry (April 1880–June 1885) resorted to coercion in Ireland, but also passed a Land Act in 1881 which seriously infringed the principle of freedom of contract between landlords and tenants. However, Gladstone's attempt to undermine support in Ireland for the Home Rule movement was a failure, and in the 1885 general election, the first under the system of household suffrage for the counties (which had tripled the Irish electorate), the Parnellites won 85 out of 103 Irish seats. Already, Gladstone had reached the conclusion that the existing system of British rule in Ireland was untenable, and in April 1886, soon after forming his third ministry, he brought forward a bill to establish a legislative assembly in Dublin with responsibility for Irish affairs, although Ireland was to remain within the United Kingdom. This plan was rejected by the House of Commons in June, after lengthy debate, when some ninety-four Liberal MPs rebelled against their own leader and voted with the Conservatives, securing an adverse majority of thirty. A mixture of genuine ideological objections to Irish Home Rule (arising principally from fears for the security of the empire) and anti-Irish prejudice, made it impossible for the Westminster Parliament to agree to a bold change of policy for which, it has to be said, Gladstone had allowed himself little time to prepare men's minds.[22]

In crucial respects, the conduct of the Conservative Party can be seen as a triumph for those traditional parliamentary opposition tactics aimed at effecting a disintegration of the governing party. Lord Salisbury had spurned Gladstone's private communications advocating a bipartisan settlement of the Home Rule question – although it is hard to see how Salisbury could have induced his party to swallow such an agreement, even if he had wanted it – and instead ruthlessly exploited the opportunity to smash the Liberal hegemony, just as the Liberals, forty years before, had used the repeal of the Corn Laws to destroy Peel's Conservative Party. It was noticeable, for instance, during the parliamentary debates on the Home Rule bill, that the Conservatives were happy to take a back seat, allowing dissident Liberals like Hartington, Goschen and Chamberlain, to give the lead in denouncing Gladstone's plan. Such a tactic, of course, was deliberately designed to accentuate the division in the Liberal ranks. Furthermore, it was made clear at an early stage that the Conservatives were willing to enter into an electoral arrangement with the dissident Liberals, whereby the leadership promised to use its influence to prevent Conservative candidates being put up, at the next general election, against Liberal MPs who had shown the courage of their convictions by voting against Gladstone's bill.[23]

The general election held in the summer of 1886, following the defeat of Gladstone's Home Rule bill, inevitably served to intensify the feelings of bitterness and betrayal caused by the defection from the Liberal Party of the dissidents, who now called themselves Liberal Unionists. By and large, the electoral pact between the Conservatives and Liberal Unionists held firm, but in many constituencies Liberal Unionists found themselves confronted with opposition from Gladstonian Liberal candidates. At Bath, for example, Edmond Wodehouse had to withstand a Gladstonian Liberal challenge, and he wrote afterwards to a Liberal Unionist colleague:

> How bitter the old Parliamentary hand [Gladstone's nickname] has been against us! and what letters and telegrams he has despatched in endeavours to upset us! Never again ought any of us to regard him as other than an opponent whom we should exclude from power so far as lies in us. I, for one, am utterly disgusted with his unscrupulous demagogy.
>
> He has been well beaten; but this is the only first battle of a campaign; and until the campaign is ended – until we have finally crushed the old gentleman's sinister projects, I hope our alliance with the Conservatives will continue unbroken.[24]

In the initial stages of the great Liberal schism, most Liberal Unionist MPs still hoped that it would be possible to bring about a reconciliation with the main body of Liberals, provided Gladstone and his Home Rule commitment could be removed from the picture. Given Gladstone's advancing years (he was 77 in December 1886), and the not unjustifiable belief among Liberal Unionists that it was only his authority and prestige that had induced the majority of Liberals to reluctantly go along with his Irish scheme, the notion that Gladstone and Home Rule might soon be shelved was not entirely unrealistic. Whatever the prospects of Liberal reunion may have been in the months following the 1886 general election, however, Gladstone's remarkable longevity and resilience ensured that the commitment to Irish Home Rule survived as the main plank of his party's programme for the next few years, and in this way any chance of reconciliation with the Liberal Unionists was killed off. The diary of one Liberal Unionist MP, Arthur Elliot, details the consequences of Gladstone's determination to preserve his Home Rule policy, in terms of the increasing ferocity and bitterness of parliamentary debates, particularly when the Liberal Unionists found themselves obliged to support the Salisbury government's alternative Irish policy of renewed coercion. On 2 May 1887, Elliot noted how he himself was engaged in a violent clash with Gladstone, who 'seemed to lose all self-control'. Elliot also recorded how the Home Rule controversy poisoned the social life of the London clubs: the most notorious case, early in 1887, involved the Reform Club, where the rival Gladstonian and Liberal Unionist members were blackballing each other's nominations for new members. By the end of the torrid 1887 session of Parliament, therefore, the idea of Liberal reunion was becoming a distant dream, and it was increasingly likely that the Liberal Unionists' ultimate destiny lay in a closer relationship with the Conservative Party.[25]

The long-term consequences of the polarisation of British politics, brought about by Gladstone's adoption of the Home Rule cause, are well illustrated by Hugh Berrington's analysis of division lists given in the table below, which is a continuation of the figures cited earlier (see Table 5.1):[26]

Table 5.2   *Voting behaviour in the House of Commons*

Year	Number of divisions	True Two-party votes (%)	Cross-bench votes (%)	Extremist votes (%)
1871	209	38	38	24
1881	170	49	16	35
1883	194	35	20	45
1890	208	65	28	7
1894	214	84	5	11
1899	318	75	20	5
1903	225	86	6	8

During the final decade of the nineteenth century, then, a two-party alignment, with 90 per cent or more of MPs of both main parties following their party's line in whip divisions, is evident in well over one-half of the divisions, and at times the figure exceeded four-fifths. The effect of the Home Rule crisis, in other words, was to put an end to the practice of substantial co-operation between the party front benches, and to substitute for it a system more similar to that which we know today, where the two dominant parties are normally found opposing one another in the division lobbies. Dissident voting by moderates (cross-bench votes) still fluctuated to a considerable extent, but was often far lower than in the pre-1886 period. More striking still is that the table shows a dramatic decline in the amount of dissident voting by 'extremists'. What was happening here was that the party leaderships were becoming more closely identified with their back-bench followers, so that there were far fewer occasions when those on the far left or far right of the political spectrum chose to rebel against their leaders (though of course such revolts never disappeared entirely). In fact, the process whereby party voting became the norm at Westminster was more rapid, and complete, on the Conservative side than it was with the Liberals. As early as 1890, dissident voting of any kind on the Conservative benches had virtually disappeared. Liberal voting conformity was not quite so fully developed, but then the Liberals were inherently a somewhat fractious party representing a wide range of opinions, and the problem was exacerbated by the fact that the elderly Gladstone rarely attended the House of Commons, except on important occasions, making party discipline more difficult to enforce.[27] It was still possible for a Liberal government to collapse, as did Lord Rosebery's in June 1895, because of radical abstentions in the division lobby (see Doc. 30). As for the Liberal Unionists, it has recently been shown that their voting became more consistent during the Parliament of 1892–95, when their alliance with the Conservatives was consolidated by the experience of being in opposition to the Liberal governments of Gladstone and Rosebery.[28]

A further contribution to the development of partisan behaviour at Westminster was being made, in the mean time, by the House of Lords. It is true that the Upper House had usually been dominated by the Conservatives during the reign of Victoria, but, as we saw in chapter 1, the Lords was generally careful not to take its opposition to Commons' measures to extreme lengths. The 1870s and early 1880s did, however, see some signs of a growing assertiveness on the part of the Lords, including the rejection in 1880 of the Gladstone government's Irish Compensation for Disturbance bill, and in 1884 Salisbury used the Conservative majority in the Upper House as a lever with which to force Gladstone to agree to a bipartisan settlement of the franchise and redistribution question. This tendency towards a more aggressive stance against the policies of Liberal governments was naturally encouraged by the Liberal schism of 1886, which resulted in the majority of Liberal peers eventually abandoning their party,[29] and it culminated in the Lords' rejection of Gladstone's second Home Rule bill, in September 1893, by the record margin of 419 votes to 41. From Salisbury's point of view, the success of the Upper House in resisting Gladstone's plan represented a triumph for the referendal theory of the peers' constitutional rights, which he had been evolving since the 1860s. According to this theory, it was the duty of the House of Lords to oppose measures sent up from the Commons when it was clear that the government of the day had no electoral mandate for its policy, so that the government would have to decide whether to refer the matter to the electorate by requesting a dissolution of Parliament. In this way, Salisbury sought to present the Lords as the protectors of the rights of the people, against a House of Commons which was allegedly becoming so servile to the party machine that it often did not accurately represent public opinion. The general elections of 1895 and 1900 both produced large Conservative majorities, apparently vindicating the conduct of Salisbury and his fellow peers in 1893. In his own time, it may be argued, Salisbury was successful in partially rehabilitating the House of Lords as a political power, but in doing so he encouraged an attitude of intransigence which led to disaster during the constitutional crisis of 1909–11.[30]

The paradoxical fact about the House of Lords, in the late nineteenth century, is that its undoubtedly enhanced political prestige served to mask its failure to evolve into a really effective second chamber. For instance, a new system of standing committees, designed to provide a better scrutiny of bills, was soon abandoned, and Salisbury's own plan to rejuvenate the membership of the Upper House, through the introduction of life peerages, was never adopted. The efficiency of the House of Lords as a revising chamber was hampered by the fact that most important government legislation was not sent up from the Commons until the last month or so of the parliamentary session, leaving little or no time for proper examination by the peers. This perhaps helps to explain why so few peers attended at Westminster on a regular basis, or made the effort to speak when they did come, with the result that sittings were often concluded within an hour or two. Clearly, the ineffective working of the Upper House was merely compounded by such slackness, so that a vicious circle was created. The House of Lords, therefore, proved to be much better at butchering Liberal legislation than in helping to improve it.[31]

An inevitable consequence of the prominent role played by the 'Irish Question' in late-Victorian politics, and of the high levels of partisan behaviour at Westminster generated by it, was the tendency for governments to assume greater control over the House of Commons by regulating its procedures. In 1882, the obstructionist tactics pursued by the Parnellites and the Fourth Party necessitated a special autumn sitting of Parliament to consider procedural reform, one of the ideas adopted being the closure (or *clôture*), whereby the Speaker of the House of Commons was empowered to bring a debate to an end if this was the 'sense' of the House. Five years later, furious Irish resistance to the Conservative government's new Coercion bill led to the adoption of the 'gag', or 'guillotine', which enabled the government to set a time limit for debate on a particular bill, after which a division had to be taken. These new procedural devices came to be employed on a regular basis by governments of both parties, the Liberals, for example, using the guillotine to force through their second Home Rule bill in 1893. The 1880s and 1890s also witnessed a significant growth in government domination of the parliamentary timetable. In theory, only two days per week were set aside for government business, but it became common for ministers to appropriate further time for their measures by means of special resolutions, applying only to one session at a time, but the regular use of which meant that in practice late-Victorian governments were claiming precedence for their business on four days of each week. This situation was finally regularised in 1902, when the standing orders of the House of Commons were changed.[32] In the partisan atmosphere of the late-Victorian Parliament, with governments claiming ever greater control over the proceedings, it is easy to see why the confrontation between government and opposition should have become a permanent feature of political life.

It is no coincidence that the political disruption caused by the Home Rule crisis was accompanied by efforts to set on a new footing the relationship between the party leaders and their extra-parliamentary organisational bases. With regard to the National Liberal Federation, Joseph Chamberlain's opposition to Gladstone's Irish policy ended in his losing control of his own creation, at a conference in May 1886, and it is interesting to note that some fifty constituency Liberal associations affiliated to the NLF for the first time once it was in the hands of Gladstone's supporters. It was at this point that the NLF truly became the *National* Liberal Federation, and its headquarters were moved, symbolically, from Birmingham to London. 1886 also saw a re-structuring of the Conservative National Union (following on from the settlement of the dispute between the National Union and the Conservative leaders in 1883–84), and a change in its rules of affiliation so that it became a more comprehensive and representative body. Both these organisations were now officially recognised by the party hierarchy, rather than being instruments for furthering the ambitions of particular factions or individuals, and leading figures like Gladstone and Salisbury were to be seen addressing their respective annual conferences in the years that followed. Thus, in yet one more respect, leaders and followers were being drawn closer together.[33]

******

The position of the Liberal Unionist Party makes an interesting case-study of the realities confronting a 'third party' in British politics (leaving aside the Irish Nationalists) towards the end of the nineteenth century. In contrast to the Peelites of mid-century, the Liberal Unionists found that systematic attention to party organisation in all its forms was essential for political survival. There were, for instance, officially recognised Liberal Unionist whips operating in the House of Commons, and meetings of the parliamentary party were held several times per session. More-over, the political climate of the time meant that it was necessary for the Liberal Unionists to establish an extensive network of extra-parliamentary organisations, and to maintain it through regular public meetings. A Liberal Unionist Association (LUA) was set up in London, in the midst of the Home Rule crisis in 1886, and helped to co-ordinate the party's campaign during the general election of that summer. Subsequently, much effort was put into increasing the number of local associations connected to the LUA by sending out travelling agents to provide advice and encouragement, and the situation by February 1888 was that the

LUA had 115 affiliated branches covering 257 constituencies.[34] The LUA literature department was responsible for distributing millions of pamphlets and leaflets annually, and there was also a monthly party newspaper, the *Liberal Unionist*, which achieved a circulation of about 10,000. In a report written at the end of 1888, the chief whip, Lord Wolmer, stated that the LUA's 'annual expenditure is now between 8 & 9 thousand, & might be profitably increased to 10' (one would have to multiply these figures by about 40 to convert them to 1990s money values). Some of the heaviest items of expenditure included '6 organising agents at work in the Country paid from £250 to £500 a year. I should like to employ 4 more', and 'a large staff of lecturers paid from a guinea a lecture to £50 a month', whose travelling expenses also had to be met. 'Subsidies to weak kneed Associations', as well as the cost of fighting by-elections, were also mentioned.[35] A Liberal Union Club was opened in London in the spring of 1887, and one of its initiatives was to finance a number of 'Union Jack vans', which were sent out to tour the electorally important rural areas where the Gladstonian Liberals were also very active. Leaflets, flags and other paraphernalia were thus distributed, the rear of each van could be used as a platform for making speeches, while there was also lantern equipment so that the crowds could be entertained with images of the Royal family, Unionist politicians, or the latest outrages committed in Ireland.[36]

Attendance at party gatherings all over the country, as well as at the annual conference held in London each December, constituted a heavy additional burden for senior Liberal Unionist politicians, but 'stumping' the country was now an unavoidable part of the political process. The *Annual Register*, in its accounts of each year's main political events, seemed to weary of the incessant flow of words pouring forth from public platforms, but it is significant that the Liberal Unionists were reported as displaying more energy than the other parties in their determination to keep in the limelight, and that the patrician leader, Lord Hartington, proved to be a powerful and effective orator.[37] One amusing sign of the times was the way that even Liberal Unionist peers, like the Earl of Selborne and the Earl of Northbrook, emerged in a new and unsuspected light as hard-hitting public speakers, while the Duke of Argyll displayed a talent for writing patriotic verse to be sung by Scottish audiences (see Doc. 12).

All of this Liberal Unionist activity was designed to buttress the position of a party seeking to preserve itself as an independent entity within Parliament. Though there could be no question of any *rapprochement* with the main body of Liberals, so long as Gladstone and his Home Rule policy remained, and though it was true that the Liberal Unionists ultimately owed their electoral survival to the forbearance of the Conservatives in not running candidates against them, it would still have been too much of a wrench, emotionally as well as politically, for the Liberal Unionists to throw in their lot with the Conservatives.[38] On two occasions, in July and December 1886, Hartington therefore declined Salisbury's proposal that a coalition government be formed with Hartington as Prime Minister. Instead, the band of seventy-eight Liberal Unionist MPs preferred to offer a general independent support to a Conservative administration headed by Salisbury, in the knowledge that, although the Conservatives lacked an overall majority in the House of Commons, they could survive provided the Liberal Unionists did not vote against them on critical occasions. The Liberal Unionists in fact chose to sit on the opposition benches as a way of asserting their claim to be the true heirs to the Liberal tradition. They also displayed their independence, from time to time, by voting against the Conservative government on certain issues, or else by abstaining (see Doc. 29), and no doubt a sense of electoral expediency mingled here with any genuine attachment to Liberal principles. This arrangement lasted for the duration of the 1886–92 Parliament, and from the Conservatives' point of view it had one great advantage, in that they were able to avoid provoking the considerable back-bench resentment which would undoubtedly have existed if a coalition had taken place on the generous terms offered by Salisbury in 1886.[39] Formal coalition had to wait until June 1895, when circumstances were very different: the two parties had been drawn closer together by their opposition to Gladstone's second Home Rule bill, and it was now clear that there was no way back to the Liberal Party for the Liberal Unionists. Salisbury took the premiership for the third time, and four posts in the new Cabinet were alloted to Liberal Unionists.

******

To conclude this study of British parliamentary politics during the Victorian period, it is worth posing the question whether the triumph of partisanship should be regarded, on balance, as a sign of success or of failure? It was certainly a failure from the point of view of aristocratic politicians such as Lord Kimberley, cited earlier in this chapter, who would have regretted the breakdown of the more consensual style of politics which had encouraged tacit co-operation between the two party front benches. (Kimberley himself, it is interesting to note, remained a Liberal after 1886, in spite of his scepticism about Gladstone's Home Rule policy.) Equally, however, the injection of a greater degree of partisanship into British political life could be seen as a sign of a healthy polity, in which Parliament had adapted itself to the requirements of a mass-participatory system by engaging the enthusiasm and passion of large numbers of ordinary people. The proliferation of extra-parliamentary political organisations during the last two decades of the nineteenth century, the Primrose League being the most impressive example, attests to this more optimistic assessment of developments.

It is also important to consider the significance of the way in which a partisan system of parliamentary politics came to be firmly established, as this may tell us a great deal about the relationship between Parliament and society. As we have seen, a strong case can be made for regarding the Home Rule crisis of 1886 as the critical event in the process of polarisation, but this raises awkward questions concerning how representative Parliament was of the aspirations and anxieties of the British electorate. After all, it is far from clear that the 'Irish Question', in itself, was of great interest to the majority of the British people, except perhaps in certain areas of the country like Lancashire and Clydeside, where a populist brand of Protestantism, inspired by resentment against Irish Roman Catholic immigrants, was influential. In the 1886 general election, for example, one Liberal Unionist MP, representing a Devonshire constituency, thought that the hostility towards him of many Liberal voters had less to do with the merits of the Home Rule issue, as it did with the fact that he had voted against Jesse Collings' amendment favouring allotments for agricultural labourers.[40] Further evidence of the indifference of many British voters towards anything involving Ireland may also be detected in the pattern of low turn-outs which was a feature of the general elections between 1886 and 1900.[41] If this really was the case, then we need to ask ourselves why the parliamentarians became so obsessed with a subject which bored much of the electorate? Some historians have gone so far as to virtually imply that the Home Rule controversy provided a smoke-screen which enabled the politicians to avoid having to address the more pressing social questions of the day like poverty and unemployment. It was the political elite at Westminster, in other words, who decided that Ireland was to be the contentious issue of late-Victorian politics.[42] No doubt this is an overly-cynical interpretation of what happened, for it was scarcely possible for Gladstone and other political leaders to simply ignore the presence of eighty-six Irish Nationalist MPs, returned at the 1885 general election, more especially since this group effectively held the balance of power at the opening of the new Parliament. Parliamentary circumstances dictated that the 'Irish Question' had to be confronted, one way or another.

These observations suggest that there was no simple, direct link between British society and its Parliament. However much energy had to be expended by the politicians in attaching to themselves the support of millions of electors, there was never any question of the electors imposing their specific priorities on Westminster politics. Paradoxical as it may seem, the late-Victorian Parliament managed to respond to the challenge of a mass electorate by polarising itself, but it did so on an issue that was not of pressing concern to many voters. Politicians like Gladstone even introduced the language of 'class' into their rhetoric, attributing the opposition to the Home Rule bill to self-interest on the part of the 'upper ten thousand'.[43] But this was a very different version of the 'class war' from that beginning to emerge in certain areas of British society, where conflicts between employers and trade unions, and the spread of various types of socialist thought, were beginning to make an impact. The potential problem facing the British Parliament by the end of the nineteenth century, therefore, was that it risked getting stuck in a political groove, created by the Irish Question, from which it might not easily be moved.

Notes

1 Gary W. Cox, *The Efficient Secret: The Cabinet and the Development of Political Parties in Victorian England* (Cambridge, 1987), pp. 91–112. There was also a sharp drop in uncontested elections, in 1868, especially in the English boroughs: T. O. Lloyd, 'Uncontested seats in British General Elections, 1852–1910', *Historical Journal*, VIII (1965), pp. 260–5.

2 For party organisation generally, see H. J. Hanham, *Elections and Party Management: Politics in the time of Disraeli and Gladstone*, 2nd edn., (Brighton, 1978); E. J. Feuchtwanger, *Disraeli, Democracy and the Tory Party* (Oxford, 1968).

3 John Vincent, *The Formation of the British Liberal Party, 1857–68* (London, 1972 edn.), pp. 244–67: H. C. G. Matthew, *Gladstone, 1809–74* (Oxford, 1986), pp. 103–48.

4 Nancy E. Johnson (ed.), *The Diary of Gathorne Hardy, Later Lord Cranbrook, 1866–1892* (Oxford, 1981), 23 February 1872; T. A. Jenkins (ed.), *The Parliamentary Diaries of Sir John Trelawny, 1868–1873* (Royal Historical Society, Camden Fifth series, vol. 3, 1994), 24 February 1871, 19 March 1872, 31 July-1 August 1873; and see generally, Agatha Ramm, 'The Parliamentary Context of Cabinet Government, 1868–1874', *English Historical Review*, XCIX (1984), pp. 739–69.

5 Hugh Berrington, 'Partisanship and Dissidence in the Nineteenth Century House of Commons', *Parliamentary Affairs*, XXI (1968), p. 344.

6 *Ibid.*, pp. 349–53.

7 See Richard Shannon, *The Age of Disraeli, 1868–1881* (London, 1992), pp. 97–9, 116–18, for the whole of this paragraph.

8 T. A. Jenkins, *Gladstone, Whiggery and the Liberal Party 1874–1886*, (Oxford, 1988), pp. 74–6, 144–51.

9 Northcote's diary, 26 April 1880, in Andrew Lang, *Life, Letters and Diaries of Sir Stafford Northcote, first Earl of Iddesleigh*, 2 vols. (London, 1890), ii, 150.

10 For the Conservatives, see Johnson's introduction to *The Diary of Gathorne Hardy*, pp. xxxiii–iv. For the Liberals, see Hartington's letters to Gladstone, 25 July 1875, 10 February 1876, 3 April 1876, 19 February 1877, 5 August 1878, 8 May 1879, 29 June 1879, BL Add MSS 44144, fos 184, 196, 208, 218, 271; 44145, fos 13, 17. The diary kept by Lord Ripon, between December 1878 and April 1880, BL Add MSS 48641–3, suggests that meetings may have become larger and more frequent in this later period.

11 Jenkins, *Gladstone, Whiggery and Liberal Party*, pp. 39–50.

12 *Ibid.*, pp. 51–101; Richard Shannon, *Gladstone and the Bulgarian Agitation 1876*, 2nd edn., (Brighton, 1975); Marvin Swartz, *The Politics of British Foreign Policy in the Era of Disraeli and Gladstone* (London, 1985).

13 This is the central theme of Ann P. Saab, *Reluctant Icon: Gladstone, Bulgaria and the Working Classes, 1856–1878* (Harvard, 1991).

14 Hartington to Granville, 26 November 1876, PRO GD 30/29/22A/2.

15 Hartington to Granville, 21 September 1879, *ibid.*

16 Jenkins, *Gladstone, Whiggery and Liberal Party*, pp. 102–40.

17 Roland Quinault, 'The Fourth Party and the Conservative opposition to Bradlaugh, 1880–1888', *English Historical Review*, XCI (1976), pp. 315–40. For the whole of the following discussion, see R. F. Foster, *Lord Randolph Churchill: A Political Life* (Oxford 1981).

18 Sir John Mowbray, *Seventy Years at Westminster* (London, 1900), pp. 294–5.

19 Peter Marsh, *The Discipline of Popular Government: Lord Salisbury's Domestic Statecraft, 1881–1902* (Brighton, 1978).

20 Jenkins, *Gladstone, Whiggery and Liberal Party*, pp. 198–229.

21 Ethel Drus (ed.), *A Journal of Events During the Gladstone Ministry 1868–1874 by John, First Earl of Kimberley* (Royal Historical Society, Camden Third series, vol. 90, 1958), 8 December 1868.

22 For the Irish Home Rulers, see David Thornley, *Isaac Butt and Home Rule* (London, 1964); Conor Cruise O'Brien, *Parnell and his Party* (Oxford, 1964). For a sympathetic treatment of Gladstone's move towards Home Rule, see H. C. G. Matthew (ed.), *The Gladstone Diaries*, X (Oxford, 1990), pp. xcviii–c, cx–clxi.

23 Marsh, *Discipline of Popular Government*, pp. 109–12.

24 Wodehouse to Arthur Elliot, 16 July 1886, NLS MSS 19487, fo. 255.

25 Elliot's diaries for 1886–7, *ibid.*, 19512–13.

26 Berrington, 'Partisanship and Dissidence', p. 344. In the figures for 1899 and 1903, the Liberal Unionists are included among the Conservatives. Similar findings are made by John D. Fair, 'Party voting behaviour in the British House of Commons 1886–1918' *Parliamentary History*, V (1986), pp. 65–82.

27 *Ibid.*, p. 348. Michael Barker, *Gladstone and Radicalism: The Reconstruction of Liberal Policy in Britain, 1885–94* (Brighton, 1975), pp. 170–2.

28 John D. Fair, 'From Liberal to Conservative: The Flight of the Liberal Unionists after 1886', *Victorian Studies*, XXIX (1986), pp. 291–314.

29 Gregory D. Phillips, 'The Whig Lords and Liberalism, 1886–1893', *Historical Journal*, XXIV (1981), pp. 167–73.

30 Corinne C. Weston, 'Salisbury and the Lords, 1868–1895', *Historical Journal*, XXV (1982), pp. 103–29.

31 Andrew Adonis, *Making Aristocracy Work: The Peerage and the Political System in Britain 1884–1914* (Oxford, 1993), especially chapter 3.

32 Peter Fraser, 'The Growth of Ministerial Control in the Nineteenth Century House of Commons', *English Historical Review*, LXXV (1960), pp. 444–63.

33 P. C. Griffiths, 'The Liberal Party and the Caucus in 1886', *History*, LXI (1976), pp. 183–97; Marsh, *Discipline of Popular Government*, pp. 57–9, 198–204.

34 *The Liberal Unionist*, October 1888, pp. 35–6.

35 Wolmer to Lord Hartington, 10 December 1888, Devonshire MSS (Chatsworth House, Derbyshire), 2nd series, 340.2201.

36 *The Liberal Unionist*, December 1888, p. 79, July 1892, p. 239.

37 *Annual Register*, 1888, pp. 177–9, 223; 1889, p. 182; 1890, p. 225.

38 T. A. Jenkins, 'Hartington, Chamberlain and the Unionist Alliance, 1886–1895', *Parliamentary History*, XI (1992), pp. 108–38.

39 Marsh, *Discipline of Popular Government*, p. 113.

40 Lord Ebrington to Earl Fortescue, 29 June 1886, Fortescue MSS (Devon RO, Exeter), 1262M/FC55.

41 Neal Blewett, *The Peers, the Parties and the People: The General Elections of 1910* (London, 1972), pp. 20–3.

42 A. B. Cooke and John Vincent, *The Governing Passion: Cabinet Government and Party Politics in Britain, 1885–86* (Brighton, 1974), pp. 3–9, 458.

43 T. A. Jenkins, *The Liberal Ascendancy, 1830–1886* (London, 1994), pp. 221–2.

Chronology

November 1830 Resignation of the Duke of Wellington's Tory administration, replaced by Earl Grey's Whig government which passes the Great Reform Act in 1832. A general election late in 1832 produces a vast majority for Grey's party.

July 1834 Grey retires, succeeded by Viscount Melbourne.

November-December 1834 King William IV, alarmed by the government's Irish policy, dismisses Melbourne and his colleagues. Sir Robert Peel forms a minority 'Conservative' administration, and issues his 'Tamworth manifesto', declaring his intention to govern in a spirit of moderate reform.

April 1835 In spite of gains at a general election, held early in the year, Peel is still in a minority and finally resigns. Melbourne returns to office.

June 1837 Death of William IV, accession of Queen Victoria. This necessitates a general election, held in August, which weakens the position of Melbourne's government.

August 1841 A decisive election victory for the Conservatives brings Peel back to office. From 1842 onwards he pursues a policy of Free Trade, involving substantial reductions in the level of tariffs.

1845 Friction between Peel and his party erupts when one-half of Conservative M.P.s oppose his attempt to conciliate Ireland by increasing the state grant to the Roman Catholic seminary at Maynooth. Peel relies on opposition support to carry his measure.

November-December 1845 The impending famine crisis in Ireland, caused by the failure of the potato crop, prompts Peel to abandon the defence of the Corn Laws. Unable to carry his Cabinet colleagues, Peel resigns, but Lord John Russell fails to form a Liberal government because some of his colleagues are also unhappy about repealing the Corn Laws. Peel re-forms his government now pledged to the policy of repeal.

May-June 1846   The repeal of the Corn Laws is carried, with Liberal assistance, but over two-thirds of Conservative M.P.s, led by Bentinck and Disraeli, oppose Peel. Shortly afterwards, 69 Conservative rebels join with the Liberals to defeat Peel's Irish Coercion bill, forcing him to resign.

June 1846   Russell's weak Liberal government not helped by a general election in 1847. Russell receives independent support from Peel (until his death in June 1850) and his band of followers, the 'Peelites', such as W. E. Gladstone.

February 1852   Fall of Russell's government, replaced by the Earl of Derby's minority Conservative administration, led in the House of Commons by Disraeli. A general election in the summer does not alter the Conservatives' position.

December 1852   Derby resigns. The Earl of Aberdeen forms a Liberal-Peelite coalition. Britain enters the Crimean War, against Russia, in March 1854.

January-February 1855   Aberdeen's coalition is censured by the House of Commons over its inept management of the Crimean expedition, and resigns. Derby fails in an attempt to bring Palmerston and some Peelites into a Conservative ministry. Finally, Palmerston forms a Liberal government, but is not supported by leading Peelites. Crimean War ends in April 1856.

March-April 1857   Palmerston is defeated in the House of Commons over the China War by a combination of Conservatives, Peelites and radicals. Parliament is dissolved, and the general election produces a large majority for Palmerston.

February 1858   Palmerston resigns after he is defeated by a similar hostile combination, over the Conspiracy to Murder bill. Derby forms his second minority Conservative government.

June 1859   Conservatives still in a slight minority, after general election gains. Liberals, Peelites and radicals unite (the Willis's rooms meeting), and defeat the government on a vote of 'no confidence'. Palmerston forms his second Liberal ministry.

143

October 1865 Palmerston dies in office, having just secured a general election victory. Earl Russell (formerly Lord John) succeeds as Prime Minister, with Gladstone as Leader of the House of Commons.

June 1866 Russell resigns after the defeat of his Reform bill by a combination of Conservatives and rebel Liberals ('the Adullamites'). Derby forms his third minority Conservative government, and carries the second Reform Act in 1867.

February 1868 Derby retires, succeeded by Disraeli.

December 1868 Disraeli resigns after a heavy general election defeat. Gladstone forms his first Liberal ministry.

March 1873 Gladstone resigns after the defeat of his Irish University bill. Disraeli declines to form another minority Conservative government, and forces Gladstone to return to office.

February 1874 Disraeli forms his second ministry after a decisive election victory for the Conservatives. Gladstone retires from the Liberal leadership in January 1875, replaced by Granville and Hartington.

November-December 1879 Gladstone's first campaign in Midlothian, denouncing the policies of Disraeli (cr. Earl of Beaconsfield, 1876).

April 1880 Large Liberal majority at the general election, Gladstone (supplanting Granville and Hartington) forms his second ministry. Major problems posed by the rise of the Irish Home Rule Party, led by Charles Stewart Parnell.

November 1884 The third Reform Act is carried, following private negotiations between the Liberal and Conservative leaders.

June-December 1885 Gladstone's ministry resigns after a defeat on the budget. The Marquis of Salisbury forms a minority Conservative government. At the end of the year, a general election results in a hung Parliament, with the Irish Home Rulers holding the balance.

January-June 1886 The Liberals and Home Rulers combine to turn out Salisbury's government. Gladstone forms his third ministry. In April he brings in a Home Rule bill, but it is defeated in June by a combination of Conservatives and rebel Liberals (Liberal Unionists).

July 1886 After a general election the Conservatives are the largest party, but they lack an overall majority. Salisbury forms his second ministry, kept in power with independent support from the Liberal Unionists, led by Hartington and Chamberlain, who decline to join a coalition.

144

July 1892 Gladstone forms his fourth ministry after a general election which left the Liberals as the largest party, but dependent on Irish support for a majority. Gladstone's second Home Rule bill is rejected by the House of Lords in September 1893.

March 1894 Gladstone retires, succeeded by the Earl of Rosebery.

June-July 1895 Rosebery's divided government resigns after the Secretary for War is censured by the House of Commons (the cordite vote). Salisbury forms a coalition government of Conservatives and Liberal Unionists, which secures a large majority at a general election.

October 1900 Salisbury's government secures a renewed electoral mandate, taking advantage of the popularity derived from its (apparent) success in conducting the Boer War.

Selected documents

Document 1

In February 1852 Queen Victoria opened the first session of Parliament to be held in the new Palace of Westminster, built after the fire of 1834. The opening took place only two months after Louis Napoleon's *coup d'état* in France, a coincidence that served to heighten the British sense of pride in their parliamentary institutions. From the *Illustrated London News*, 7 February 1852.

> The annual opening of the Session of the high Parliament of Great Britain is always an event of European as well as of national interest. At the present strange crisis of the world's history, when, with some trifling exceptions, it is the only free Parliament in Europe, its solemn inauguration is of more than usual importance. This old Parliament – the model and the envy of nations – meets for the first time in a new edifice; but it meets on the old historical site, and, let us trust, with the old historical spirit, determined to maintain the Country which it represents in its old and high position, free and independent at home, respected abroad by every other nation that aspires to be free, and dreaded only by the enemies of human rights and the real progress of civilisation.

Document 2

E. M. Whitty was one of the first parliamentary sketchwriters, contributing a weekly column to *The Leader*. His observations about the House of Commons are of particular interest because he was a radical, not prone to obsequious flattery. From *St.*

146

Stephen's in the Fifties: The Session 1852–3, A Parliamentary Retrospect, ed. Justin McCarthy (London, 1906), p. 32.

> I think they *are* 'the first assembly of gentlemen' in Europe – patricians, no doubt, but patriots, too, whose blood leaps through their limbs when there is occasion, as though they never had trafficked away small national perquisites – and who will (about midnight) cheer madly noble sentiments. But, whether or not first gentlemen in Europe, this is certain: that they are a cleverer, shrewder, more dexterous set of men than you will find elsewhere in England – House of Commons existence being in itself the most magnificent of educations, in teaching the relative importance of men and things . . . MPs are accustomed to measure intellect by its exact results on the world, and capable of seeing at a glance through any pretence that may be offered by a virgin orator.

Document 3

A view of the House of Commons at the end of the nineteenth century, from a Conservative who had been an MP from 1853 until his death in 1899. Sir John Mowbray, *Seventy Years at Westminster* (London, 1900), pp. 106–7.

> There is, and always has been, a very real feeling of fraternity within the walls of the House. If a man is willing to learn and willing to work, he is recognised as a real recruit, and is welcomed accordingly. He comes in contact with other men, he respects their opinions, he discards some of his old prejudices, he gradually falls into line, and is ready to associate himself with his compatriots in the great work of legislation. Mr. Bradlaugh was a notable instance of a man who, representing the most advanced opinions, came in and dwelt among us, and earned the respect of all by his constant labours and the honest and independent expression of his views.

Document 4

The life of a busy MP in the 1830s. Edward Baines was elected for Leeds, in 1834, and wrote the following 'Journal' towards the end of his first session in the House of Commons. In addition to representing a populous industrial constituency, Baines was also concerned with issues affecting Yorkshire as a whole, and, as one of the few Nonconformists in the Commons, he was deeply involved in matters affecting his co-religionists. From Edward Baines, jnr., *The Life of Edward Baines* (London, 1851), pp. 194–5.

Journal of a Week in Parliament

MONDAY. Rose at six, much refreshed by two successive good nights' rest. Read Parliamentary papers and reports till eight; from the hour of post till half-past eleven, corresponded with constituents; at twelve attended the House to present petitions, but, standing low on the ballot list, had not been called when the House adjourned at three. Attended Committees till four; House resumed at five; debate continued till nearly midnight: real business then began; continued till three in the morning, when the House adjourned. Walked home by morning twilight; pined a little after domestic comfort; soon forgot all cares, public and private, in sleep.

TUESDAY. Rose at seven; read over petitions to be printed that day; resumed correspondence after the arrival of the post with ten letters. Attended the House at half past eleven. In luck – name drawn out of the jar early, got on petitions; afterwards attended Committee till three. House resumed at five; sat till two o'clock next morning.

WEDNESDAY. Rose at seven; attended to correspondence till twelve; walked till two; applied at the Board of Trade for information respecting the repeal of duties, and at the War Office for a soldier's discharge; attended the House at five; sat till half-past eleven.

THURSDAY. Rose at half-past six; resumed perusal of Poor-law reports – quite overwhelming. (A Bill should be introduced to enable Members to read and think by steam power.) Attended the morning sitting; from thence to two Committees. The House met again at five; sat till half-past one o'c in the morning.

FRIDAY. Resumed perusal of documents at eight; attended Committee from twelve to four. The House sat at five; continued the sitting till three the next morning; a great deal of business done after midnight.

SATURDAY. Employed this day in bringing up arrears of correspondence, in taking exercise, and in reading and pondering over the copious Parliamentary bill of fare for the next week.

Document 5

Lord Stanley was a Conservative MP and the son of the 14th Earl of Derby, the Conservative leader. In his unpublished essay, 'The Member of Parliament: his position and duties. 1857', Stanley discussed some of the means by which men could make their mark in the Commons. Liverpool RO, 920 DER (15) 41/2.

Association of oneself with a single question is an expedient common to ambitious mediocrity. Thus Oliveira is known in connection with cheap wine: Spooner, with Maynooth: Brotherton, with midnight adjournments: Hume, with economy: Buxton, with slave-trade, (as Wilberforce before him): Shee & Moore with Irish tenant-right. This plan of self-advancement promotes, I suppose, permanent and posthumous reputation, but at the expense of giving the person adopting it the character of a bore at the time. It destroys a nice perception of the relative importance of things, making the person a mono-maniac, real or pretended. It is fatal to an ordinary ambition, for such men are scarcely ever selected for office. But this does not apply to the temporary taking up of a question, and bringing it forward year after year, as Lord John Russell did with the first Reform Bill, Villiers with the Corn Laws &c &c than which no method of making one's way with the House is more effective. Much, of course, depends on the selection of a subject: but unless a mere notoriety be the object in view, it is not expedient for any man to confine himself to a single subject.

For an MP to rely, for his position within the House, on following out-of-doors, is an experiment always, and from the nature of the case, full of risk. The House shows little respect, or even tolerance, for reputations made beyond its walls. Even where these reputations are unconnected with politics, it distrusts them: they form a hindrance, not a help, to the possessors' success. The House favours and really confides in, only those who have given to it the whole energy of their lives. Authors, lawyers, soldiers, enter at a disadvantage. The explanation is simple. No man who has adopted a profession likes to believe that success in that profession can be attained by those who bring to it a partial and divided attention. To the trained, thoroughbred MP it is disagreeable to see a novelist, a barrister, or a general, rivalling or beating him in his own business, after only a few years at most of practice. Still more is jealousy of this kind shown where the MP's success has been attained in extra-Parliamentary politics. Of all men who enter Parlt, none enter it at such a disadvantage as journalists or popular orators. They are regarded (the latter particularly) as a raw militia is regarded by old soldiers, or an amateur in any business by professionals. There exists an impression (and this applies chiefly to the agitator or lecturer) that to harangue riots & meetings without responsibility, without accurate discussion of details, & without reply, is rather a low form of political activity. It is so easy, so safe, and unless done more scrupulously than is usual, so unfair! The same judgment is passed, though with less severity, on journalists: and it cannot be denied but that a more rigid logic, and a more decided rejection of mere-clap trap than either the agitator or the journalist practice, is necessary at Westminster. With talents like those of O'Connell, Cobden, or Bright, not to rise is impossible: but all these men had to experience a very cold and hostile reception from the House, before they were, so to speak, naturalised there.

The policy, therefore, of entering the House as the representative, specially, of an out-doors party, is questionable. To represent a permanent interest, as that of a certain profession, a trade, or a class not commonly represented there (as Mr E. Ball does the tenant-farmers) is a different matter, and such a position predisposes the House to hear you: but this is only to possess the means of making a *status* for yourself, not to have one already. Nevertheless, it is a good commencement: as is everything which singles you out from the mass, so long as the peculiarity has nothing in it which tends to ridicule. At the present time, neither the navy, nor the medical profession, have any efficient organ in Parlt: and one who should speak effectively for either of these professions would find a place prepared for him. But he must belong to them: the House will not endure mere advocacy, even though unpaid.

Document 6

The Great Reform bill was finally carried, in June 1832, after Earl Grey's government forced King William IV to pledge himself to the creation of a large number of new peers, if necessary, in order to override the existing hostile majority in the House of Lords. Grey's letter to Lord Althorp, the leader of the House of Commons, 11 March 1832, shows how slow the Prime Minister was to accept the need for such coercion, one reason being his appreciation of the vital role played by the King, up to this point, in supporting the reform cause. Althorp MSS, British Library (provisionally catalogued).

From the beginning we were pledged to use our best efforts & to exert all our power for the success of a measure, which we deemed of vital importance to the best interests of the Country. That obligation has been increased by the circumstances to which I have alluded [the opposition from the Lords], & by the almost unanimous support of a generous & confiding People. To the King we owe all that men can owe for the firm, unequivocal & uncompromising support which he has given us throughout.

We are bound then equally by a loyal regard for the King, by the duty which we owe to him & to the Country, & by the consideration of our own honour, not to shrink from any measure which all these interests prescribe, under a firm conviction of its wisdom and necessity. ... [but] As at present advised, I do not think anything could induce me to be a consenting party to a large creation of Peers.

Document 7

The tactical complexities of parliamentary reform, in 1866. On 15 January the Liberal chief whip, Henry Brand, wrote to W. E. Gladstone, leader of the House of Commons in Earl Russell's government, recommending that a Franchise bill be introduced without an accompanying redistribution of seats. It should be noted that there had been a dissolution of Parliament in the summer of 1865. BL Add MSS 44193, fo. 147.

I fear that if we deal with seats, as well as with the franchise, we shall get into trouble, as we did in 1860.

Members representing places under sentence will of course turn against us; and every member will be voting with the halter of a dissolution round his neck, for we must dissolve, if places are disfranchised, whereas, it is not absolutely necessary, if persons only are enfranchised.

A separate franchise bill was introduced, but it faced criticism from various Liberal quarters because of the omission of any plan for redistribution. Lord Grosvenor, one of the so-called 'Adullamites', who were hostile to reform, moved an amendment to the second reading of the bill calling for the production of a redistribution scheme before the House of Commons agreed to any change in the franchise. On 22 March Brand sent the following memorandum to Gladstone, *ibid*, fo. 155.

There are three classes of disaffected Liberals whom it is important to secure, & who may be secured.

1stly Men who, although opposed in their hearts to Reform, do not desire a change of Govt.

2ndly Men who doubt whether the Govt really intend to deal with seats at all.

3rdly Men who believe that the Govt in dealing with seats will act under the influence of [John] Bright.

The 1st Class would be secured by a stout attitude on Grosvenor's motion. It should be treated as a *vital question*.

The 2nd & 3rd Classes would be secured by a promise to produce a seats Bill before we go into Com[mitt]ee on the Franchise Bill.

To dissolve upon Reform in the present temper of the Country would not improve our position. Should the feeling of the Country be roused in the next three weeks, we need not concern ourselves about a Dissolution, for that very feeling would carry the second reading of the Bill.

In the event, Grosvenor's amendment was narrowly defeated by 318 votes to 313, and the second reading carried on 27 April. A redistribution plan was subsequently introduced. But the Adullamites and the Conservatives succeeded in defeating the franchise bill during the committee stage, on 18 June, leading to the government's resignation. The outside agitation by the Reform League, manifested in the 'Hyde Park riots' of July, thus came too late to help the Liberal government.

Document 8

Two reactions to the unexpectedly decisive Liberal election victory in 1880. Reform of the county franchise had been one of the main issues on which the Liberals campaigned. Their strong performance extended even to the small boroughs, likely to be the victims of any redistribution bill transferring seats to the larger boroughs, the Liberals' traditional strongholds.

(*a*) Frederic Harrison, radical thinker and writer, to the radical MP Sir Charles Dilke, 5 April 1880, BL Add MSS 43898, fo. 179.

... this is a soldier's battle, a radical – and a cultivated radical – victory ... any Liberal Ministry must be pledged to deal with *redistribution* in this House.

Unless this is done, there will be a swinging back again some day, and in 1886 the old trick of 1874 will be played over again. The Tory is only stunned, he must be killed. And not only killed, but put in his coffin, and not only put in his coffin, but screwed down, and a brass plate nailed on the top. The only way to screw him down is redistribution ...

(*b*) Lord Salisbury to the Conservative leader, Lord Beaconsfield (formerly Disraeli), 7 April 1880. Salisbury's comment about the small boroughs is particularly interesting given the line he took on redistribution during the negotiations with Gladstone, in November 1884, which secured the passage of the third Reform Act. Hughenden MSS (Bodleian Library, Oxford), B/XX/Ce/139.

The elections have been a puzzle to me – & I have seen no cause which satisfactorily accounts for so sudden a change. I suppose bad harvests & bad trade have done the most. I suppose a sick man who makes no progress is apt to change his doctor, though the doctor may not be at fault: & the mass of borough voters know that they are pinched – & nothing more. I have not gone into the statistics – but I suspect this election will finally dispose of any interest the Conservative party are inclined to take in the existence of the small boroughs. The question will soon come before us: as County franchise will be one of their first subjects of legislation.

Document 9

In the years after the second Reform Act of 1867, which enfranchised many working men in the boroughs, there was a growing feeling that the character of politics was inevitably being changed. Lord Halifax, a former Liberal Cabinet Minister, to his fellow aristocratic 'Whig', Lord Fortescue, Christmas Day, 1877, Fortescue MSS (Devon RO, Exeter), 1262M/FC 126.

... I am convinced that many of us old public men must make up our minds to see public questions dealt with in a very different fashion from the days of our youth. The people generally were ignorant in those days & the old Whigs were far in advance of the people. ... Now the people are more educated – all public questions are freely and universally discussed in the press as soon as they can be considered and before they can be taken up by the heads of parties. It may not be wise to *say* it, but in practice it cannot be helped. Public opinion will direct the course of public men – it may to a great extent be formed by them – but able writers in the public press will do much more than any man can do in Parliament.

Document 10

Another 'Whig' view, this time from a serving Cabinet Minister, Lord Kimberley, to the Viceroy of India, Lord Ripon, 3 September 1881, commenting on the way the depression, affecting agriculture and parts of industry, was leading to calls for a return to the protectionist policies abandoned in the 1840s. BL Add MSS 43522, fo. 269.

Incessant rain is destroying the harvest, and the prospects for next winter are not cheering. The probable break down of the French Commercial Treaty [of 1860] is bringing about a certain agitation for 'fair trade' i.e. our old friend Protection. The farmers will vote for this to a man ... I am not at all sure some of the artisans will not join them, & the Tories are already beginning to coquet with this anti-Free Trade movement.

However what Demos may do, I think the wisest man cannot foretell. What seems pretty certain is that he is sure before long to veer round entirely. Uncertainty and instability are a growing danger in English politics.

Document 11

The protracted general election campaign of 1885, fought under the new system created by the third Reform Act, was notable for Joseph Chamberlain's attempt to impose his programme of radical policies upon the Liberal Party. The following extracts from the diary of the 15th Earl of Derby (the Lord Stanley of Document 5), who had joined the Liberals in 1882, record the reactions to Chamberlain's campaign, and the uncertainty as to the likely behaviour of the new electors. Liverpool RO, 920 DER (15).

9 September 1885 [Chamberlain's speech at Warrington, outlining his programme] chiefly remarkable for its evident object, which is to drive all moderate Liberals out of the party, or at least out of the direction of it, and reorganise it on an exclusively radical basis. He goes further in the direction of socialism than any man of his political rank and standing has done yet, but for the most part his language is so vague and general that he has pledged himself to nothing definite.

16 October 1885 There has never been in my recollection such a continued rhetorical battle: nearly all the leading public men have been 'on the stump' as the phrase is, and many of them half a dozen times ... many people whose interest in politics is moderate do not care to read incessantly repeated arguments on the same topics. Of Chamberlain's three proposals – free education, purchase of land by Local Authorities, and graduated taxation – the first is on the whole popular rather than otherwise, the second is generally condemned, and the third, which indeed is extremely vague, has scarcely been discussed, or treated as a practical suggestion.

23 November 1885 [First day of polling] Nobody knows in the least what to expect. The Conservatives during the last ten days have been in better spirits, thinking that the cry of 'Church in danger' is telling in their favour, and also that Chamberlain's semi-socialist programme has helped them: but it is all guesswork, and it is re-membered that scarcely any one guessed right either in 1880 or in 1874.

In the event, the Liberals did less well than anticipated, and this was a serious set-back to Chamberlain's ambitions.

Document 12

Aristocracy and populist politics. The 8th Duke of Argyll, a Liberal Unionist, wrote the following verses to be sung at political meetings during the 1892 general election campaign. Fiercely critical of Gladstone's policy of Home Rule for Ireland, Argyll stressed the bonds between Scotland and Ulster. Smith of Jordanhill MSS (Strathclyde Regional Archives, Glasgow), TD1/356.

Men of Ulster, Scotsmen too,
we shall not leave you in the hands
of men who hate both us and you,
and all the Union of our lands.

We have no right to cast you off
and if we had, we shan't.
Let those who laugh and try to scoff
assail with axe the hardy plant.

Of British races firmly set
on Irish soil by you and us;
you'll make them know the danger yet
of selling Ulster's freedom thus.
[etc.]
Chorus
We have no right to cast you off
and if we had, *we shan't*!

Document 13

The defeat of the Speaker. Following the general election of 1835, Sir Charles Manners Sutton failed to secure re-election to the post of Speaker of the House of Commons, being defeated by James Abercromby, who had the support of the opposition Liberal leaders. In effect, the vote was a trial of strength between the opposition and the Conservative government of Sir Robert Peel, which had been controversially appointed in December 1834 after King William IV dismissed Lord Melbourne's government. Peel was finally forced to resign, in April 1835, after further serious defeats in the Commons, and the Liberals returned to office. From the diary of Richard Potter, radical-Liberal MP for Wigan, 19 February 1835, BLPES, COLL MISC 146, vol. IX.

The second Reformed Parliament met this Day in the former house of Lords which has been filled up for the Commons since the frightful Fire on the 16th of October last. At two o'clock we were summoned to the House of Lords (the former painted chamber) where the Commission for opening the Session was read, on our return Lord Francis Egerton rose to propose Sir Chas Manners Sutton as Speaker. Sir Chas Burrell seconded the Nomination.

Mr W. Denison proposed the Right Honble James Abercromby, Mr Ord seconded the Nomination.

A debate ensued – a little after six o'clock the Division took place when the numbers were

For Sir C. M. Sutton 306
Against him   316
Majority against
Sir Charles   10!

156

The question was then put that Mr Abercromby be called to the Chair which was carried without a Division!!

I voted against Sir C. M. Sutton for Speaker, and in favour of Mr Abercromby because a great *public Principle* was at issue, Sir Charles M. Sutton is a rank Tory and the Right Honble Jas Abercromby a Reformer, and I think the Speaker should be chosen from that party in the House which predominates.

Besides Sir C. M. Sutton had been in constant communication with the Duke of Wellington and Sir Rob Peel and the other Ministers at a most critical period on the formation of the Ministry, and when it was determined to dissolve the late Parliament. Sir Charles was not altogether impartial. . . .

This was the largest division ever known in the annals of Parliament, there being 624 members divided, including the 2 Tellers. Two Members paired off, and 32 Members absent, makes the total number of Members 658.

It is a little singular that a majority of the English Members present were in favour of Sir Charles Manners Sutton – the numbers being

For Sir C. M. Sutton	259	
Against him	225	34
Irish and Scottish		
Members for Sir C. M.	47	
Against	91	44
	622	

Document 14

Problems of party management in the 1830s.

(*a*) Lord Granville Somerset was one of those MPs who gave informal assistance to the Conservative chief whip, Sir Thomas Fremantle, in securing the attendance of MPs at the opening of each session of Parliament. On 3 January 1839 he wrote to Fremantle returning the draft of the proposed circular to be sent out to MPs. Fremantle MSS (Bucks RO), D/FR/111/2/5.

> I think the letter as a *publick* letter will do very well. I enclose you also a list of the MPs to whom I can write privately. To some of the names I have put Queries as I think you may prefer writing to them yourself. But now comes the Question, what shall I say to my correspondents? Of course I shd urge them to be in attendance by all sorts of general reasons & so forth; but have you ever consulted Sir R. Peel on the propriety of asking our friends to

meet at his House on the morning (say 12) of the 5th of February? It may be difficult to tell them anything *precise*; but He will have his followers *more in Hand* by talking to them generally, than if they go into the H of C without a previous meeting, & without some apparent consultation. Now I conceive the great object is to have our friends under *very good control*, so as to wield them without difficulty.

(*b*) When the idea of a meeting was put to Peel, he threw cold water on it, writing in a tone that illustrates very well his personality. Peel to Fremantle, 9 January 1839, *ibid.*, D/FR/111/2/39.

> ... I am sure it is not a good thing to have general meetings – without some specific object – and still less to make a meeting at my house, at which I might have nothing to say, a pretext for calling persons from the Country.
>
> It is so obvious that a full attendance at the commencement of the session is most desirable – it is so uncertain whether an amendment to the address may not be unavoidable – that every person of common sense must understand *first* that it is desirable he should be in his place, and secondly, that it is utterly impossible to give him an assurance before hand, that there will certainly be a division.
>
> To get up a meeting not otherwise called for, merely to justify a very urgent letter to a few idle men, would not in my opinion be good policy, and would transfer to me personally, their complaints of being called up to Town without a necessity for it – that is, according to their Construction of necessity.

Document 15

Cross-party voting in the House of Commons in the 1840s. The diary of Sir John Cam Hobhouse, a front-bench Liberal, shows firstly, how Sir Robert Peel's Conservative government was defeated on its Factory bill, when Lord Ashley carried an amendment reducing the working limit to a 10-hour day (though this amendment was later rescinded), and secondly, how the Liberal opposition helped the government to pass its Dissenters' Chapels bill (designed to protect the rights of Unitarians), which was opposed by many Conservatives. BL Add MSS 43746.

18 March 1844 [Ashley's amendment carried by 8 votes] There was no distinction of party in this vote – ninety nine Conservat-

ives voted with Ashley – and about 50 Liberals, chiefly radicals &
free traders with Govt: Russell, G. Grey, Howick and Palmerston
[all front bench Liberals] voted with Ashley – Labouchere, F. Baring
& myself with Governt. Ministers confessed they were surprised
with the result ... They reckoned upon Russell's support, & indeed considering his conduct on prior occasions on this question
they had a right to do so. The Melbourne Cabinet unanimously
opposed the 10 hours bill of Michael Thomas Sadler and were
supported by Conservative leaders ...

28 June 1844 Went early to H of C – voted with Govt. for 3rd
reading of the dissenters chapels bill ... we were 201 to 81 – of the
majority 112 were Liberals – of the minority 6 were Liberals –
another great vote carried by opposition.

Document 16

Two Conservative MPs claiming their right to 'independence',
when opposing Peel's government in 1844 over its Sugar Duties
bill. Peel's plan to reduce the differential between the duties levied
on foreign sugar, and on that from British colonies in the West
Indies, was seen not only as harmful to the colonies but as having
wider implications for the principle of agricultural protection for
British farmers. Many Conservatives therefore opposed their
leader on this issue, though they repudiated the idea that this
meant they were disloyal to Peel generally. 17 June 1844, *Hansard's
Parliamentary Debates*, 3rd series, LXXV, cols 1031–2, 1045–8.

> *Lord Sandon* As to the general aspect of the Ministry, he must take
> that opportunity for expressing the deep and sincere attachment
> which he felt towards the Government of his right hon. Friend,
> than whom there was no man more able or better fitted to hold
> the reins of power ... it was with extreme regret he had heard
> him declare that whoever did not vote with him upon all occa-
> sions he could consider in no other light than as having thereby
> tacitly given a vote indicating a want of confidence in him. Such
> a system of Government had never yet been tried in this country
> ... Notwithstanding, therefore, he was an habitual and a firm
> supporter of the right hon. Gentleman's Administration, he was
> resolved that nothing should hinder him from voting as an
> independent Member of that House.
>
> *William Miles* He could assure the Government that he held the
> high Conservative principles they professed; but, at the same time,

he reserved to himself the right of exercising his judgment freely and independently. Did the Government conceive that the character of the party would be raised, if those who maintained the same opinions, but who still differed from them on questions of detail, obsequiously followed every move they took?

Document 17

A dramatic occasion in the House of Commons, on 15 May 1846, when the third reading of the bill to repeal the Corn Laws was carried. The Conservative Prime Minister, Peel, was opposed by the majority of his own party, including Benjamin Disraeli, and relied on support from Lord John Russell and the Liberals. Within a month, 69 Conservative MPs had joined with the Liberals to bring down Peel's government by defeating its Irish Coercion bill. From the diary of the front-bench Liberal, Sir John Cam Hobhouse, 15 May 1846, BL Add MSS 43748.

I went to the H of C after dinner . . . & found Disraeli speaking against the Corn bill. His arguments were the old ones – but well put. His conclusion for a good twenty minutes was a studied phillipic against Peel – which was very powerful indeed & produced a great effect in all parts of the house. Peel looked miserable & his brother Jonathan more wretched still . . . even Macaulay told me he thought the effect very powerful & the best Disraeli ever made. Russell who followed was unable to go on for some time on account of the prolonged cheering . . . Peel got up after Russell and talked in terms of ill affected contempt of Disraeli, more than hinting he had been a candidate for office in 1841 – & saying, truly enough, that if D had thought so badly of all Peel's career why did he support him up till 1844. However Peel spoke in a manner not usual with him and on one occasion was completely put out by a charge which conveyed no obscure hint of disbelief in his honour both personal & political. He stopped – looked round & stopped again – then seemed to try to speak – but was choked & his eyes full of tears . . . I never saw him *beat* before – and much as I dislike him & disapprove his conduct I felt much distressed – and so did others of our front [bench] opposite him. However he went on tolerably well though in a lower tone than usual. He made no allusion to Russell's reproof of his having kept back his opinions too long – nor did he say a single civil thing of our party. On the whole the speech was a failure – though much cheered by our friends when he sat down . . .

It was said our majority was above 100 – but it was 98 ie 327 to 229. There was great cheering when the numbers were announced . . . The house adjourned at four & a quarter [a.m.]. I went home in broad daylight. And so this protection Parliament (house of commons) has voted & passed by a great majority the total repeal of the Corn Laws!! No living soul could have done this but Peel & I am not surprised at the increasing rage of the protectionists. They appear more angry than ever.

Document 18

After the fall of his government, in June 1846, Peel adopted an independent position in the House of Commons. He was prepared, when necessary, to give support to Lord John Russell's Liberal ministry (which lacked an overall majority in the Commons), since the Liberals were committed to maintaining the policy of Free Trade, and Peel was anxious not to see the formation of a protectionist Conservative government. However Peel was unwilling to act as the leader of an organised 'third party', although there was a group of 'Peelite' MPs committed to his Free Trade policy, and, it was argued, many other Conservatives who would follow Peel's lead if only he would give one. This was the opinion of Sir John Young, who had been the Conservative chief whip between 1844 and 1846, and who did his best to act as a 'Peelite' whip thereafter. On 22 February 1850 he wrote to Peel once again, urging him to act. This followed a division in the House of Commons, the previous day, in which Russell's government had only been able to defeat a vaguely worded protectionist motion, relating to agricultural distress, by 273 votes to 252, a majority of just 21. The 'Peelites' had been split on this occasion. BL Add MSS 40603, fo. 92.

On last night 35 of your friends voted in the minority, 28 (yourself included) in the majority. So that without your assistance the Government was defeated by 7.

I enclose a list marked – on looking it over you will see the 35 & 28 are mostly men of considerable local influence, good fortune, and high character. They form an important body, and will cast the balance to whichever party they may eventually incline.

They will stand by free trade, they are the men who carried the repeal of the Corn and Navigation laws, and will steadily maintain that policy – but they have no sympathies with and no confidence in the present Government – they are with you, not with Lord J. Russell.

These two lists, about half as many more absent, and nearly an equal number favourably inclined but generally voting with the Protectionists – say about 160 – would rally round you personally, or any organization distinctly formed under your auspices and guided by your advice – but they will not make sacrifices and risk their seats, night after night, & year after year, for those whom they cannot help regarding as political opponents. I do not believe that any active opposition is contemplated, but support will no doubt be withheld, and without such support the Whigs have no command of a majority . . .

I do not speak of any defection of the Radicals – though 30 of them are rumoured to be hostile to the Government . . . Such a defection would of course precipitate events – but even without it I should not be surprised at seeing the Government in great difficulty.

I mention this because so large a number of men have sought communications with me in the course of the last week – probably not fewer than 60 or 70. And from all I can gather, if a Protectionist Government is to be averted by any arrangement, and your Commercial policy receive fair play for some years to come during its infancy and this period of transition, you yourself are the only person able or likely to effect these objects.

Young's plea was made in vain, however, and a little over three months later Peel was dead, following a riding accident.

Document 19

The problems of opposition in the 1850s. Sir John Pakington, a front-bench Conservative, complaining to the chief whip about the lack of communication between the party leaders. At the time of Pakington's letter, Lord Palmerston was at the head of a 'patriotic' Liberal ministry, conducting the war effort against Russia in the Crimea. It should be remembered that the autumn was usually a quiet time, politically, as Parliament was not normally in session. Pakington to Sir William Jolliffe, 11 November 1855, Hylton MSS (Somerset RO), DD/HY/18/11/20.

I saw some of our colleagues in London, but they did not seem to know much, except Stanley – I had some interesting talk with him. I have not heard anything of Dizzy since I left London, & probably shall not.

I am told he out of humour.

Our party is conducted on the peculiar principle of nobody ever communicating with anybody, and that it should remain a party under such circumstances is a remarkable proof of the influence of English politics & the strength of party ties ...

But with all our mismanagement & our difficulties I think we might hope soon for brighter days if we could only have a little better concert amongst ourselves.

Document 20

More problems of opposition in the 1850s. In December 1857 an emergency session of Parliament was summoned, at a time when a financial crisis had rocked the City of London. The Conser-vative leader in the House of Commons, Disraeli, attacked the Palmerston government for failing to take immediate action, but he was defeated by the humiliating margin of 295 votes to 117. The following report from a junior Conservative whip to the chief whip, shows that there was much discontent with Disraeli's 'opportunist' style of leadership, especially at a time of national emergency. Edward Taylor to Sir William Jolliffe, 'Sunday night' [13 December 1857], Hylton MSS (Somerset RO), DD/HY/24/21/5.

As it is most probable I shall not see you before I leave London, I think it well you should know the result of my observation taken among 'our flock' yesterday and today – all with whom I have spoken, without an exception, are angry, sulky, or otherwise dis-satisfied with our division on Friday night, and there can be no doubt the move we made has only tended materially to strengthen Ministers, and exhibit our own want of union.

I enclose an analysed list of numbers and names, by which you will perceive that *four* men only, not our own, voted in the minority. The absentees, on whom we have a certain fair right to reckon, count 72 – and those who went with the Chancellor [of the Exchequer], over whom we consider we have some lien, are 35 in number ...

My impression now is that another adverse division, *of our own seeking*, will be fatal to the coherence of our party in the H of C and I venture that the only policy that remains, however distasteful

163

to an eager leader like Disraeli, is *not* again to *attack* till times and circumstances alter, but content ourselves with fighting in *defence* only.

It is too late now to complain – but I sincerely wish we had avoided *dividing*, when it became evident that all those who we expected to befriend us from the other side were *dumb*, and either from pressure of constituency, whip of Hayter, or blind idolatry of Palmerston, would not venture to follow the dictates of their own expressed opinions, and vote for the amendment.

. . . the majority against us would have been quite fractional, if our own men had only come up, and acted together; but it is because no pressure or persuasion we can bring to bear will ensure that very desirable result, that I beg & entreat you will represent to Disraeli that to accustom the members we call 'our party' to vote in this disjointed manner, is virtually to disgust, & break them up – and however it may be adverse to his own inclinations to sit inactive on the front opposition bench, he has really not any choice left, but must if he cares for his own authority, and our continued existence, *bide his time*.

In fact, Disraeli did not have to bide his time for long, as in February 1858 the Conservatives were able to seize an opportunity to turn out Palmerston by combining with disaffected Liberals and Peelites to defeat the Conspiracy to Murder bill.

Document 21

In February 1858 Lord Derby formed his second minority Conservative government. At the end of the 1858 session, the Liberal MP Edward Knatchbull Hugessen made the following observations in his diary. The 'independent Liberals' were radicals hostile to the idea of Lord Palmerston returning as Prime Minister. Diary 30 July 1858, Brabourne MSS (Kent RO), U951/F27/1.

Lord Derby's Government is still in power, and stronger than when he accepted office this spring, mainly from two reasons. One, an ill-advised and premature attempt to oust them [by attacking their policy in India]; the other, the Liberal course they have adopted, which has conciliated many of the 'independent Liberals', altho' it has displeased the Ultra Tories, and will not unlikely, in the long run, cause a split in the Conservative camp which will prove fatal to the Government. It was, however, in my opinion, necessary to their existence as a Government that they should show themselves more Liberal in office than in opposition, and it is advantageous to Liberal Principles that they should have been in office this year: it may even be well that they should continue in office for a longer time. There are certain questions which could hardly have been solved by a Whig Cabinet, but which have now found their solution. For instance, the admission of the Jews to Parliament ... The Property Qualification for Members of Parliament has also been abolished with the consent of Parliament, to the great chagrin and disgust of the Conservative Country Gentlemen, who divided against the Bill, but in vain. The Liberal tendencies of the Government are a genuine blow to these Gentlemen, who have always been the main strength of the Tory Party, and who are now beginning to find the old traditions of their Party slipping away from them one by one, almost imperceptibly, and their leaders among the first to renounce them. There are rumours of Lord Derby being 'a second Peel' in his betrayal of his Party, but I believe that the great majority of the Conservative Country Gentlemen have too much good sense not to see that the world cannot stand still, and that this may be the last chance Lord Derby will have of showing that 'Conservative Progress' is a possibility ... Personally, I am not sorry to see Lord Derby in power, for the Whigs have had a good long spell of office, and a change will do them good. The state of the Liberal Party has been anything but satisfactory of late ...

Document 22

One of the most intriguing aspects of the politics of the early 1860s was the collusion between the Liberal Prime Minister, Lord Palmerston, and the opposition leaders, which at times resulted in a virtual 'truce' in party warfare. The object of the Conservative leaders was to encourage Palmerston to resist pressure from radicals in his party, such as John Bright.

(a) Palmerston to Queen Victoria, 27 January 1861, reporting a conversation with Lord Malmesbury, who was acting as a secret intermediary. The Conservatives were particularly concerned, at this point, with the policies of the Chancellor of the Exchequer, W. E. Gladstone. A. C. Benson and Lord Esher (eds.), *The Letters of Queen Victoria, 1837–1861*, 3 vols. (London, 1907), iii, 429.

[Malmesbury] said that he was charged by Lord Derby and Mr. Disraeli with a message similar to that which he had conveyed last year, namely, that if Mr Gladstone were to propose a democratic Budget making a great transfer of burthens from indirect to direct Taxation, and if, the Cabinet refusing its concurrence, Mr. Gladstone were to retire, the Conservative Party would give the Government substantial support except in the case of the Government wishing to take an active part in war against Austria. This did not of course mean an abstinence from usual attacks and criticisms in debate, but that no step would in such case be taken to produce a change of Government. In fact, said Lord Malmesbury, neither the Conservative leaders nor the Party wish at present to come into office, and have no intention of taking any step to turn the present Goverment out. Mr. Bright had indeed proposed to Mr Disraeli to join together with the Radical Party, the Conservatives, for the purpose of turning out the present Government; and especially to get rid of Viscount Palmerston and Lord John Russell. Mr Bright said he would in that case give the Conservative Government a two years' existence, and by the end of that time the country, it might be hoped, would be prepared for a good and real Reform Bill, and then a proper Government might be formed.

This proposal, which it must be owned was not very tempting, Lord Malmesbury said had been declined . . .

(*b*) The 'pact' at work. Thomas Sotheron-Estcourt, a front-bench Conservative, recorded an occasion on which the Conservatives came to the government's rescue by helping to defeat a radical motion criticising Palmerston's conduct as Foreign Secretary, in 1839, when the Afghan War broke out. Diary, 19 March 1861, Sotheron-Estcourt MSS (Gloucester RO), D1571/F411. Brand was the *Liberal* chief whip, Whitmore a junior Conservative whip.

Full House. Brand fetched Whitmore & Disraeli – who pulled the Government through a most awkward scrape of Ld Palmerston mutilating despatches . . .

(*c*) However, the 'pact' was not always operational. The diary of Edward Knatchbull Hugessen, now a junior Liberal whip, shows how the parliamentary situation was changed by Gladstone's success in forcing through the repeal of the paper duties. It serves to emphasise just how precarious was the political balancing act performed by Palmerston, who did not want a complete breach with Gladstone and the radicals. Diary, 17 May 1861, Brabourne MSS (Kent RO), U951/F27/1.

Since I last wrote in this book, the complexion of affairs has been some what changed. Both Locke King's & Baines' [county and borough] franchise bills were defeated, the 2nd reading of the Church Rates Bill was only carried by a small majority, & the Radical Party became more & more dissatisfied with the Government, which they accused of lukewarmness to Liberal measures, & of relying upon the support of the Conservative opposition. But Gladstone changed everything by his Budget . . . The Radicals were delighted. At once they renewed their allegiance to the Government, & extolled Gladstone to the skies. The Conservatives are angry, & less disposed to support us than before, but circumstances will probably cause us to tide safely over the session.

Document 23

The problems of a Liberal chief whip. By 1871 Gladstone's Liberal ministry, which had carried a number of major reforms, was losing political momentum. One of its measures was the Army Regulation bill, which abolished the system whereby army commissions were purchased, but the generous compensation it offered to current commissioned officers was disliked by many radicals, and on 25 May 1871, during the bill's committee stage, it only survived by a majority of 16 votes. The chief whip, George Glyn, reported to Gladstone on 27 May, explaining the difficulties he was having in managing the party. BL Add MSS 44348, fo. 100.

I send you an analysis of the Division & I have come to the conclusion that I am not free from blame for what occurred & that there is less fear than I thought for the future of the Bill, it is at the same time painful & pleasant to feel this, but you must I think come to the conclusion I have, that there is a large margin, in the list of those who were *not away on purpose*, upon which to work on the next occasion. I sent out as strong a whip as the nature of the amendment for Thursday seemed to require, but where I failed was in an early knowledge of the fact that with a large body of men *in London* I had not got them *into the House*, and a fatal delay in hunting them up. I speculated too much upon absentees, who had not appeared, coming down later in the evening. I did not check the return of the dinner pairs & I find in this I lost *many men*, some of whom might have been hunted up between 10 and 12 o'clock. Still it is not to be denied that great apathy does exist & it will be difficult to get a *large* majority upon this Bill . . .

Document 24

Henry Brand, a former Liberal chief whip, was Speaker of the House of Commons from 1872 until 1884. In the following extract from the diary which he kept during his Speakership, he notes the beginning of the Irish Home Rulers' deliberate policy of obstructing parliamentary business, something that was to be a prominent feature of parliamentary politics for years to come. Sir Stafford Northcote had become leader of the Commons in 1876, when Disraeli was raised to the peerage; Lord Hartington had been leader of the Liberal opposition since 1875, when Gladstone had gone into (temporary) retirement. Brand's diary, 14 August 1877, HLRO, Hist Coll 95, vol. VII.

The Session has been long, but has not borne much legislative fruit. The programme of the Govt in the Queen's speech at the beginning of the session was humble, & its modest promises have not been in all cases performed.

The Session would have been tranquil & orderly but for the introduction on the part of a limited knot of Irish Members of the tactics of obstruction.

Obstruction has played a conspicuous part in our proceedings. It reached its climax on the famous occasion when the House (in Committee) sat for 26 hours, & when ... we were very near suspending seven members! I am very glad that this extreme measure was not resorted to: but undoubtedly, if the tactics of obstruction are again renewed in the same aggravated form, the H[ouse] must take severe measures, otherwise it will decline in public credit. There are even now hints that the Irish will renew their obstruction in a more active form next session ...

Northcote's management as Leader has improved. He is very candid & fair & has won the confidence of the House which relies upon him for dealing plainly with them.

His weakness lies in an undue apprehension as to his own supporters. He has sometimes given way, when he ought to have controlled them.

Mr Disraeli had a strong hand over his party; but Northcote has yet to attain that command.

Hartington has made great way not only with his own supporters, but also with Ministerial Members. He improves too in speaking. But the Liberal Party does not gain in cohesion, and the advent of their return to power seems more distant than ever.

Document 25

A dissident 'Whig' back-bencher of the early 1880s. W. C. Cartwright, a landowner, was a not-so-young member of a group sometimes referred to as the 'young Whig party', because of the prominent part played in it by youthful members from aristocratic backgrounds. These 'Whigs' were unhappy with the land legislation introduced by Gladstone's second ministry in response to the growing power of the Home Rule movement in Ireland. During the 1880 session there was much criticism of W. E. Forster's hurriedly prepared Irish Compensation for Disturbance bill, which even many members of the government disliked, and which was eventually rejected by the House of Lords. In 1881, the 'Whigs' succeeded in extracting a number of concessions from the government when the Irish Land bill was being debated. From the diary of W. C. Cartwright, Cartwright MSS (Northants RO), 6/14–15.

> *3 July 1880* Cotes one of our whips, a man of great sense, spoke to me of the importance that the moderate ... men on our side should make forceful representations as to the dissatisfaction entertained by a section of the party at the measures brought forward by the Government. Unfortunately Gladstone holds no general intercourse with men in the House. He comes in from behind the Speaker's chair – sits on the Treasury bench – conferring with Bright or Forster – never going amongst the members generally – and what is still more deplorable, consulting at home only with his own familiars. He acts on the impulse of his own consciousness and with intensified impulsiveness. I feel sure that we are threatened with a fall.

> *17 June 1881* [After the government had only narrowly defeated a Whig amendment to the Land bill.] Last night's division has produced a considerable impression. Thirty-six Liberals voted against Government while about fifteen who had paired during the dinner hour remained away so that their Conservative pairs voted ... The effect was shown by Gladstone today announcing the virtual concession of what I ask for in my amendment – direct access for landlords to the [Land] Court.

Document 26

The trials of Sir Stafford Northcote. As leader of the Conservative opposition in the House of Commons, from 1880 to 1885,

Northcote's authority was frequently undermined by the independent actions of a back-bench ginger group known as the 'Fourth Party'. Lord Randolph Churchill, the most famous member of this group, wrote the following insolent letter to Northcote on 9 March 1883. BL Add MSS 50021, fo. 79.

> In reply to your letter of today's date I have to remark that members who sit below the gangway have always acted in the H of Cms with a very considerable degree of independence of the recognized and constituted chiefs of either party; nor can I (who owe nothing to anyone & depend upon no one) in any way or at any time depart from this well-established & highly respectable tradition ...
>
> I will suggest however that 'similar embarrassments' might be avoided for the future, if the small party of Conservatives who sit below the gangway were to be occasionally informed beforehand of your intentions on any particular matter. They consider that they have during the whole of this Parliament worked harder in the H of Cms than any other members of the Party, & they know that a very considerable & widely spread body of public opinion in the Country approve entirely of the course of action which they have adopted ... [our] only fault is that at all times & by all means we have never ceased from attacking & embarrassing the present Govt.

Document 27

Contrasting views of the fateful debate and division, during the night of 7–8 June 1886, which ended in the defeat of W. E. Gladstone's Irish Home Rule bill. Both the diarists were Liberal MPs, but while Price supported his leader, Ebrington was one of the group of 'Liberal Unionists' whose defection secured the defeat of Gladstone's bill. George Otto Trevelyan and Joseph Chamberlain were the leading radicals among the Liberal Unionists. Trevelyan returned to the Gladstonian fold in 1887.

(*a*) Diary of Lord Ebrington, 7 June 1886, Fortescue MSS (Devon RO, Exeter), 1262M/FD 32.

> Went back about 11 just after Gladstone rose. The first part of his speech was not much & he drew ridiculous distinctions between promising to reconstruct & not promising not to reconstruct – but the finale was a beautiful piece of eloquence. I went out about the

middle & found Trevelyan fidgetting about the Library. He could not bear he said to hear Gladstone speak on this. Then we discussed the chances, & he thought we should have little to spare. Presently came the division & we won by 30. 341 to 311. A scene of wild excitement men cheering and groaning as at an election. The Irish very angry & very noisy. Outside though it was 1.30 there was a tidy crowd who cheered & groaned prominent men.

(*b*) Diary of Thomas Phillips Price, 7 June 1886, HLRO, MSS 113.

Gladstone wound up the debate in a magnificent speech of 1 hour and 36 minutes, the last 20 minutes of which was marvellously fine. He was immensely cheered after the Division by Parnellites and Liberals, and Chamberlain was howled at. It was a scene of the wildest excitement. But Home Rule is now to my mind an assured fact and not a very distant fact either, notwithstanding the Division.

Gladstone's speech was magnificent from beginning to end but to me it was profoundly pathetic, because I could not help feeling that I might never hear that noble voice, and action, to such advantage again. It is not given to any man to deliver such a speech as this was, twice, and at his age of course it is highly improbable. The elevation of tone and language, and the glorious intonation and variety of voice, is a thing to be remembered for all time. One's heart was full as one listened to it.

Document 28

Alliance politics. The general election of July 1886, after the defeat of Gladstone's Home Rule bill, produced a majority for the alliance of Conservatives and Liberal Unionists. The Conservatives were the largest party, with some 316 seats, but they needed the help of the 78 Liberal Unionist MPs in order to command an overall majority in the House of Commons. An obvious solution would have been the formation of a coalition government, but this raised serious problems for the Liberal Unionists, who were a diverse party including 'Whigs' like Lord Hartington (the leader), and radicals like Joseph Chamberlain for whom a coalition with the Conservatives was out of the question at this stage. In any case, many Conservatives were less than enthusiastic about a coalition, especially if it involved being led by a Liberal Unionist.

The end result was that Lord Salisbury formed a purely Conservative government, while the Liberal Unionists offered it their independent support. Aretas Akers Douglas (Conservative chief whip) to Salisbury, 17 July 1886, 3rd Marquis of Salisbury MSS (Hatfield House, Hertfordshire), series E.

> I have seen Brand [the son of the former Speaker] & several other Whigs & from what I can gather from them Hartington shows no desire to or intention of coalescing. In the first place they do not desire a split with Chamberlain & secondly they persist in their view that a Tory Govt would be stronger with their muted support *outside* the Govt.
>
> They divide the [Liberal] Unionist party as follows – 6 Salisbury 43 Hartington 21 Chamberlain 8 Gladstone – & fear that a coalition would drive the 29 into opposition . . . While the [Conservative] party would be ready to follow Lord H in the Commons, they would I know insist as far as they could on your being Prime Minister – but I am bound to say the majority would decidedly welcome a pure Conservative Govt.

Document 29

Liberal Unionism. The diary of Arthur Elliot, MP for Roxburghshire, illustrates the fact that throughout the Parliament of 1886–92 the Liberal Unionists were anxious to preserve their sense of separate identity from the Conservatives, sometimes voting against Salisbury's government and with the Gladstonian Liberals, or else abstaining. NLS MSS 19515–17.

14 May 1889 Welsh [Church] Disestablishment motion of Dillwyn's rejected by a majority of 50. I kept away from the debate and division as did a very large number of Liberal Unionists.

4 February 1891 [Defeat of Gladstone's Religious Disabilities bill, to remove remaining discrimination against Catholics] He made a magnificent speech, one of the best and most eloquent I have heard in the present Parliament. I spoke and voted on the same side. Liberal Unionists much divided. H. James, Chamberlain, Wolmer, Courtney, J. A. Bright & in all 12 voted and paired for the Bill. About 20 voted against. Hartington and a large number abstained.

18 June 1891 [Factory bill] Government beat in the House of Commons by a majority of 14 on Sydney Buxton's new clause raising age at which children may lawfully be employed in factories from 10 to 11. Three-fourths of Liberal Unionists voted against Government. Hartington and Henry James voting with them, however, in their character of *Lancashire* members: the feeling there being very strong amongst the Operatives in favour of 10. Government quite in the wrong: but I suppose felt unable to give way.

Document 30

The Conservative MP Sir Richard Temple wrote daily, detailed letters to his wife, describing the events and personalities in the House of Commons between 1886 and 1895. They fill eleven volumes, BL Add MSS 38916–26. The following extracts are taken from the letter dated 22nd June 1895, describing the famous 'cordite vote' of the previous day, when the Unionist opposition had succeeded in censuring the Liberal Secretary for War, Henry Campbell Bannerman. This vote provided the occasion for Lord Rosebery's government to resign. BL Add MSS 38926, fo. 154.

Yesterday Friday 21st, the longest day of the year, was also one of the most noteworthy days of this Parliament . . . Early in the morning the anticipated Whip came out five lined – it warned us about an important amendment in the afternoon – that was all. I went to the House at 3 with not very much of expectation . . . and in the lobby I understood that the Counting in (that is the official reckoning of those who had entered on both sides) shewed that the Government would have at any time before the dinner hour [roughly 7–10 p.m.], a majority of more than a dozen. So I thought to myself that there would be one more instance of an attack delivered that afternoon and *just missing* – the old story . . .

The division took place – official Tellers on both sides – soon after seven . . . The bursting cheer from the Conservative benches was suppressed till the figures could be read from the Chair for the motion 132 against 125 – majority against Government 7. Then the pent up cheers from our benches burst forth and the roof echoed and re-echoed again! . . . Harcourt's [Leader of the House] florid countenance had grown pale; the roses had indeed fled from his cheek; Ellis' (senior whip) countenance was a study in physiognomy! . . .

Then there is the question, *how* come a small majority for Government in the afternoon to be turned into a small majority against it, later in the evening? . . . I learn . . . that the cause must have been some disaffection among Ministerialists and could *not* have been slackness. There is the apparent fact that some twenty Ministerialists must have walked off or else must have (though in the precincts of the House) refrained from appearing in the Division Lobby. It cannot be that any of them expected that the division would come off at night; for there were abundant signs that it would come off before dinner. For some reason or other these men were discontented and shewed their discontent by absence from the division. The general cause of discontent is well known – disgust at the tardiness and feebleness of a Government distracted by faction and wanting in a working or a stable majority – and at the deadlock in which the business has fallen . . .

Bibliographical essay*

For constitutional history, H. J. Hanham (ed.), *The Nineteenth Century Constitution* (Cambridge, 1969), is an invaluable collection of documents. G. H. Le May, *The Victorian Constitution* (London, 1979), is a useful survey. It is essential, of course, that students read Walter Bagehot's classic, *The English Constitution* (London, 1867; 1963 edn., with introduction by R. H. S. Crossman). A recent study of the Cabinet, Gary W. Cox, *The Efficient Secret: The Cabinet and the Development of Political Parties in Victorian England* (Cambridge, 1987), probably exaggerates the importance of the 1857–68 period. There is a new survey of the upper House by E. A. Smith, *The House of Lords in British Politics and Society, 1815–1911* (London, 1992).

The Conservative Party has been fairly well-served by historians. Two volumes have been published as part of a Longman series: Robert Stewart, *The Foundation of the Conservative Party, 1830–1867* (London, 1978), and Richard Shannon, *The Age of Disraeli, 1868–1881* (London, 1992). The next volume, also by Professor Shannon, *The Age of Salisbury, 1881–1902*, is due to appear in 1995. There are also useful single-volume surveys by Robert Blake, *The Conservative Party from Peel to Thatcher* (London, 1985), and Bruce Coleman, *Conservatism and the Conservative Party in Nineteenth Century Britain* (London, 1988).

Until recently the Liberals had fared much less well, but three new publications may have helped to rectify the situation: Jonathan Parry, *The Rise and Fall of Liberal Government in Victorian Britain* (Yale, 1993), T. A. Jenkins, *The Liberal Ascendancy, 1830–1886* (London, 1994), and G. R. Searle, *The Liberal Party: Triumph and Disintegration, 1886–1929* (London, 1992).

* See also the endnotes to each chapter.

The following monographs have more to say than most about the parliamentary dimension to politics. Ian Newbould, *Whiggery and Reform, 1830–1841* (London, 1990); J. B. Conacher, *The Peelites and the Party System, 1846–52* (Newton Abbot, 1972); Angus Hawkins, *Parliament, Party and the Art of Politics in Britain, 1855–59* (London, 1987); E. D. Steele, *Palmerston and Liberalism, 1855–1865* (Cambridge, 1991); John Vincent, *The Formation of the British Liberal Party, 1857–68*; 2nd edn., (Brighton, 1976), is better on the grass roots than on the parliamentary party; J. P. Parry, *Democracy and Religion: Gladstone and the Liberal Party, 1867–1875* (Cambridge, 1986); E. J. Feuchtwanger, *Disraeli, Democracy and the Tory Party* (Oxford, 1968); T. A. Jenkins, *Gladstone, Whiggery and the Liberal Party, 1874–1886* (Oxford, 1988); W. C. Lubenow, *Parliamentary Politics and the Home Rule Crisis: The British House of Commons in 1886* (Oxford, 1988); Peter Marsh, *The Discipline of Popular Government: Lord Salisbury's Domestic Statecraft, 1881–1902* (Brighton, 1978); Michael Barker, *Gladstone and Radicalism: The Reconstruction of Liberal Policy in Britain, 1885–94* (Brighton, 1975).

Much of the most important work on parliamentary politics is to be found in the learned journals, and the following list is only a selection: Hugh Berrington, 'Partisanship and Dissidence in the Nineteenth Century House of Commons', *Parliamentary Affairs*, XXI (1968), pp. 338–74, is a seminal piece, as is Angus Hawkins, ' "Parliamentary Government" and Victorian Political Parties, c.1830–c.1880', *English Historical Review*, CIV (1989), pp. 638–69; Peter Fraser, 'The Growth of Ministerial Control in the Nineteenth Century House of Commons', *English Historical Review*, LXXV (1960), pp. 444–63, can be supplemented with Gary Cox's recent 'The Development of Collective Responsibility in the United Kingdom', *Parliamentary History*, XIII (1994), pp. 32–47; Norman Gash, 'The Organisation of the Conservative Party, 1832–1846. Part I: The Parliamentary Organisation', *Parliamentary History*, I (1982), pp. 137–59, should be read in conjunction with Ian Newbould, 'Sir Robert Peel and the Conservative Party, 1832–1841: A Study in Failure?', *English Historical Review*, XCVIII (1983), pp. 529–57, and D. R. Fisher, 'Peel and the Conservative Party: The Sugar Crisis of 1844 Reconsidered', *Historical Journal*, XVIII (1975), pp. 279–302; David Close, 'The Formation of a Two-Party Alignment in the House of Commons between 1832 and 1841', *English Historical Review*, LXXXIV (1969), pp. 257–77, is a useful study based on an analysis of division lists; W. O. Aydelotte's pioneering statistical work, on the Parliament of 1841–47, is represented by 'The House of Commons in the 1840s', *History*, XXXIX (1954), pp. 249–62, and 'Parties and Issues in Early Victorian England', *Journal of British Studies*, V (1966), pp. 95–114; P. M. Gurowich, 'The Continuation of War by Other Means: Party and Politics, 1855–1865', *Historical Journal*, XXVII (1984), pp. 603–31, is of first-rate importance; Agatha Ramm, 'The Parliamentary Context of Cabinet Government, 1868–1874', *English Historical Review*, XCIX (1984), pp. 739–69, is valuable for the problems of parliamentary management.

The collection of essays edited by Robert Robson, *Ideas and Institutions of Victorian Britain* (London, 1967), includes two important pieces, by D. E. D. Beales, 'Parliamentary Parties and the "Independent" Member, 1810–1860', and James Cornford, 'The Parliamentary Foundations of the Hotel Cecil'.

Students can learn much from the commentaries on parliamentary affairs provided by contemporary journalists, notably E. M. Whitty, *St Stephen's in the Fifties: The Session 1852–3, A Parliamentary Retrospect*, ed. Justin McCarthy (London, 1906), William White, *The Inner Life of the House of Commons*, [1856–71], ed. Justin McCarthy, 2 vols. (London, 1897; reprinted in 1973, with introduction by E. J. Feuchtwanger), and the several volumes produced by Henry Lucy, beginning with *A Diary of Two Parliaments, 1874–85*, 2 vols. (London, 1886).

Useful modern editions of politicians' diaries include J. R. Vincent (ed.), *Disraeli, Derby and the Conservative Party: The Political Journals of Lord Stanley, 1849–69* (Brighton, 1978), Nancy E. Johnson (ed.), *The Diary of Gathorne Hardy, Later Lord Cranbrook, 1866–1892* (Oxford, 1981), T. A. Jenkins (ed.), *The Parliamentary Diaries of Sir John Trelawny, 1858–1865* (Royal Historical Society, Camden Fourth series, vol. 40, 1990), and *The Parliamentary Diaries of Sir John Trelawny, 1868–1873* (Royal Historical Society, Camden Fifth series, vol. 3, 1994).

Index

Index